THE OUTRAGEOUS ATLAS

The Outrageous Atlas

A Guide to North America's Strangest Places

By Richard A. Rogers
and Laurine Rogers

A Citadel Press Book

Published by Carol Publishing Group

A Citadel Press Book
Published by Carol Publishing Group

Citadel Press is a registered trademark of Carol Communications, Inc.
Editorial Offices: 600 Madison Avenue, New York, N.Y. 10022
Sales & Distribution Offices: 120 Enterprise Avenue, Secaucus, N.J. 07094
In Canada: Canadian Manda Group, P.O. Box 920, Station U, Toronto,
    Ontario M8Z 5P9
Queries regarding rights and permissions should be addressed to
Carol Publishing Group, 600 Madison Avenue, New York, N.Y. 10022

Carol Publishing Group books are available at special discounts
for bulk purchases, for sales promotions, fund-raising, or
educational purposes. Special editions can be created to specifications.
For details, contact: Special Sales Department, Carol Publishing Group,
120 Enterprise Avenue, Secaucus, N.J. 07094

Manufactured in the United States of America

10 9 8 7 6 5 4 3 2 1

Library of Congress Cataloging-in-Publication Data

Rogers, Richard Anson.
    The outrageous atlas : a guide to North America's strangest places
/ by Richard Rogers and Laurine Rogers.
        p.   cm.
    "A Citadel Press book."
    ISBN 0-8065-1445-0
    1. United States—Maps, Tourist. 2. Canada—Maps, Tourist.
3. United States—Guidebooks. 4. Canada—Guidebooks. I. Rogers,
Laurine A. II. Title. III. Title: North America's strangest places.
G1106.E635R6   1993   [G&M]   93-26117
912.7—dc20   CIP
                                                           MAP

Note to Reader

Before you begin this outrageous tour of North America, we would like to clarify a few points.

This atlas is for amusement only. Although all of the places identified are real, many of the remarks about the places are utter balderdash. The maps, statistics, and commentary were designed to be humorous. However, if the intrepid traveler within you is compelled to visit any of the places listed, consult a road map or visitor center. And make local inquiries first before you attempt to visit a place. In some cases, roads and services may not be available, and some places may be on private property.

While some areas are particularly rich in unusual place-names, others have very few. In developing this atlas, we selected sets of interesting place-names from the range that is available in North America. An attempt was made to give each state and province relatively equal representation of curious names. Some states or provinces have multiple occurrences of the same place-name. In such cases, only one site was selected at random for inclusion in the text and map. There are also many interesting place-names and place-nicknames that are known locally to the people of the particular area. But for this atlas, we obtained place-names from national sources which are identified in the back of the book.

One final point. Because of cultural or promotional concerns, the powers that be in some places have changed their, well... questionable place-names, to something more enticing or respectable. Unfortunately, unusual and humorous place-names are dwindling like endangered species. Some of the place-names listed here may have changed since the publication of this book. We hope you enjoy this collection of unique place-names and the outrageous accompanying commentary.

Introduction

North America is dotted with place-names like *Saloon Gulch,
Coyote Hole, Mud Meadows, Freezeout Mountains, Stink Lake,*
and *Wetbutt Creek*. North America's explorers and pioneers
experienced hardships that had to be endured with a sense of
humor. One can imagine the mountain men, cowboys, and
pioneers visiting around their campfires, joking about the places
they had been. Living on the frontier, they could see the
"pretense" that accompanies civilization. They often used a fine
sense of wit in naming places.

Our interest in unusual place-names was aroused while
doing archaeological fieldwork in Wyoming. The crew's tents
were pitched in an abandoned uranium mining camp named
Armpit. *Armpit* was located at a slightly higher elevation than the
nearby mining camp of *Groin*. These outrageous place-names
became the topic of much discussion among the scientific crew.
Our interest piqued, we began to look for other outrageous
place-names. Much to our surprise, we found so many that we
decided to create this atlas.

In making *The Outrageous Atlas*, we celebrate the sense of
humor that went into naming the United States and Canada and
invite you to peruse the following pages for a unique look at
North America. Join us as we leave the realm of geographic
pomp and respectability, and take an outrageous tour of our
not-so-stately heritage of strange place-names.

The United States of America

Alabama

"The Heart of Dixie"

True Facts and Silly Stats

Population: 4,062,608
Area: 50,750 sq. mi.
Capital: Montgomery
Income Per Capita: $1.50
State Flower: Mint Julep
State Motto: Y'all See That Mosquito
State Food: Cotton Candy
Nightlife: Possoms and Bats
State Insect: Boll Weevil
Most Common Personal Name: Bubba
Famous Person: Hank Williams
Major Tourist Attraction: Alabama Space and Rocket Center

Outrageous Tour Highlights

Alabama embraces diversity. Once known as the "Cotton State," Alabama has a monument to the boll weevil that taught the lesson that diversity is the best defense against disaster. Today, Alabama has a varied economic base of which agriculture is but one of many components. For the tourist, Alabama offers a diversity of attractions. The state is renowned for beautiful flowers and gardens. The city of Mobile traces its founding to 1702, and has four historic districts. Mobile has celebrated Mardi Gras longer than New Orleans. However, some visitors may wish to bypass Alabama's popular attractions and experience the state's diversity in its most outrageous places.

3

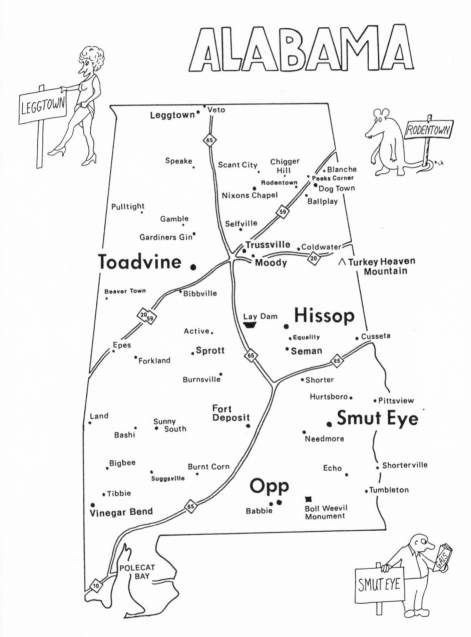

ALABAMA

Leggtown • Veto

Speake • Scant City • Chigger Hill • Blanche
Peeks Corner
Rodentown • Dog Town
Nixons Chapel • Ballplay

Pulltight

Gamble • Selfville
Gardiners Gin •

Toadvine •

Trussville • Coldwater
Moody ∧ Turkey Heaven Mountain

Beaver Town • Bibbville

Lay Dam **Hissop**
Active • • Equality • Cusseta
Epes • **Sprott** • Seman
• Forkland
Burnsville •
• Shorter
Hurtsboro • • Pittsview

Land • **Fort Deposit**
Sunny
Bashi • South **Smut Eye**
Needmore

Bigbee • Burnt Corn • Echo • Shorterville
Suggsville
• Tibbie **Opp** • Tumbleton
Vinegar Bend Babbie • Boll Weevil Monument

POLECAT BAY

Alabama, a flower of the Old South, has preserved a way of life that will enchant every visitor. Religious values are strong here. The tourist on a religious pilgrimage must visit the inspiring and uplifting *Nixons Chapel* in the northeast portion of the state. This hallowed place, between Highways 278 and 431, features such divine experiences as taped confessions that are expiated by erasures.

If a religious pilgrimage is not your idea of a good time, head north to *Leggtown*, Alabama, or south to *Beaver Town*. The voyeur may have an eye-opening stay at *Smut Eye*, Alabama. One hardly knows what to make of *Lay Dam* and nearby *Seman*, except to note that there is a need for a long shower in *Coldwater* for the namer.

Wining and dining is an unforgettable treat in the Old South. *Bibbville* and *Forkland* show that Alabama has all you need to eat. You may also want to check out the well-done cuisine of *Burnt Corn* and *Burnsville*, or the special "men's menu" at *Hissop*, while traveling scenic Highway 22.

Alabama's climate is known for its long, hot summers and mild winters. You can find *Sunny South* in Alabama. To get there, follow Highway 5 to near its junction with 43, in the southwest portion of the state.

Land lovers will be pleased to know that *Land* can be found in Alabama near the Mississippi border. To find *Land*, follow Highway 17 through *Choctaw County* until you reach local #18. *Land* is only a few miles to the north.

Alabama has a specialty "pain tour," designed for travelers with hernias. Hernia sufferers can visit *Pulltight*, go on to *Hurtsboro*, and eventually find themselves in *Trussville*. Once in *Trussville*, it is not far to *Moody*.

Visitors wishing a brief excursion might go to *Shorter* and then head south to *Shorterville* on Highway 10, near the Georgia border.

Alabama's warm climate favors a leisurely pace. However, there is one community in Alabama that breaks the norm. This is *Active*, found near the center of the state on Highway 82. *Active* athletic events and the *Active* social life draw visitors from far and wide. For a different kind of adventure, head north to *Speake,* then hurry south to *Echo.* Travelers with a gnawing desire for an extraordinary experience should scurry to *Rodentown.*

Before bidding adieu to beautiful Alabama, savor the romantic past of the Old South by an inspiring visit to *Boll Weevil Monument.* Last but not least, be sure to view the pitts at *Pittsview.*

Other unusual, often overlooked places are *Polecat Bay, Chiggar Hill, Turkey Heaven Mountain, Bigbee,* and *Bashi.*

Alaska

"The Giant Land"

True Facts and Silly Stats

Population: 551,947
Area: 570,833 sq. mi.
Capital: Juneau
Largest City: Anchorage
State Motto: Burr
State Flower: Icicle
State Animal: Brass Monkey
State Festival: Fairbanks Group Shiver
Travel Season: July 24-28
State Mineral: Rock Salt
State Food: Eskimo Pie
Famous Person: Tom Bodett
Major Tourist Attraction: Denali National Park

Outrageous Tour Highlights

Alaska is by far the largest state in the United States. It would have to be large to hold the vast scenic attractions that fill it. Snow capped mountains, imposing glaciers, huge forests, and endless expanses of wilderness tundra teeming with large game animals explain the state's attraction for tourists. Bought by the United States from Russia for less than two cents an acre, this state has yielded a bonanza of natural resources and a booming tourist industry. This atlas will provide a real alternative itinerary for tourists jaded by beautiful vistas and wildlife.

A little known wonder of nature in Alaska is *Automatic Creek* not far from from Denali National Park. *Automatic Creek*

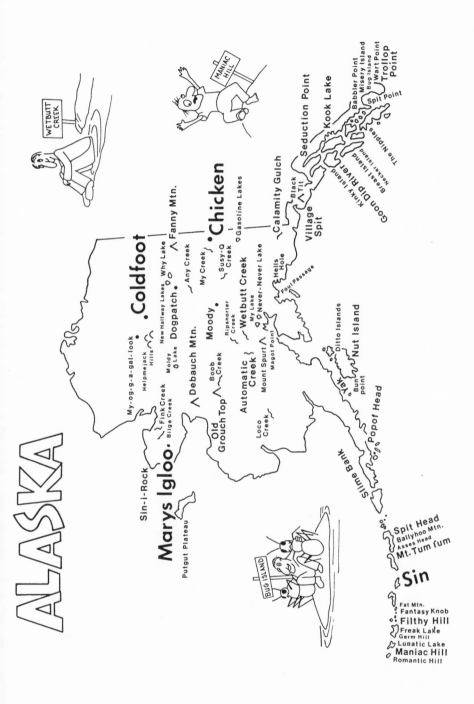

is for visitors tired of seeing creeks operated by hand. Other amazing sights in Alaska are *Mount Spurt* west of Anchorage, and *Popof Head* near Squaw Harbor. A visitor can enjoy scintillating conversation in Alaska at *Yak,* learn the art of free expression at *Babbler Point,* and get snowed at *Ballyhoo Mountain.* Intellectual tourists enjoy the open minded debates at *Asses Head* in the Aleutians.

When you take an outrageous tour of Alaska be sure to carry a few antibiotics in your knapsack before camping on *Germ Hill, Filthy Hill,* and *Slime Bank* in the Aleutians. Antifungal creams are soothing after splashing about in *Moldy Lake* in central Alaska.

Despite the state's beauty, comfort in Alaska is hard to come by, especially at *Coldfoot.* However, it is better to endure *Coldfoot* than to endure *Wetbutt Creek* in southern Alaska. You won't get away from it all at *Misery Island* on the Alaskan Gulf Coast, or find things any better at *Calamity Gulch* in southern Alaska. *Helpmejack Hills* in north central Alaska is a monument to the problem solving abilities of an early visitor.

The cold, crisp air gives Alaskans big appetites, as evidenced by *Putgut Plateau* on St. Lawrence Island. View the romantic and inspiring *Fat Mountain* in the Aleutians, especially if you are tired of gawking at anorexic topographic features in other states. *Mount Tumm Tumm,* also in the Aleutians, was an editorial comment on stomachs created by Alaskan appetites.

Eskimos have long known about a malady called "arctic hysteria," and apparently so have those who named some Alaskan places. Similarly, the long Alaskan winter nights have a deleterious effect on mental health, which the citizens of the state attempt to ameliorate with a number of different strategies. Some on the Gulf of Alaska coast drop in on *Nut Island* during the fall. Others exercise climbing *Maniac Hill.* Some shoot the rapids on *Loco Creek* with their cabin cruisers. Others soothe their nerves by bathing with rubber duckies in *Lunatic Lake.* Still others dive head first into *Kook Lake,* even when it is frozen. However, the town that best typifies the psychological character of Alaskans after a long winter is *Moody.*

Sparsely populated Alaska is inhabited by many lonely men. Their loneliness can be seen in many place-names. Get the feel of the land by visiting *The Nipples, Breast Island,* and *Black Tit* on the Gulf Coast. You should not get the idea that the men of Alaska are narrow sorts and only interested in women's breasts. *Fanny Mountain* and *Bun Point* prove they have wider interests.

No red-blooded tourist should miss *Sin,* especially the ladies of *Sin.* Many television evangelists would qualify to found a church in *Sin* but it is not good for your afterlife to die there. Apparently the locals have found a way to have moral problems with stones at *Sin-i-Rock.*

The passion pathway of Alaska starts at *Romantic Hill* in the Aleutians, goes through the *Necker Islands,* to *Seduction Point* on the Gulf coast, and ends at *Debauch Mountain* in west central Alaska. The passionate should avoid *Marys Igloo* as they will probably melt it. After a stay on *Kinky Island* on the Gulf of Alaska, you can view the incredible stuttering voyeurs at *My-og-g-a-gal-look* in north cental Alaska.

The person who named *Any Creek* in the interior of Alaska knew that if he'd seen one, he'd seen 'em all. The same for *Ditto Islands* on the Gulf of Alaska coast.

Visitors should note that Alaskans are very possessive of their geographic features. Permission is needed to fish in *My Creek* or boat on *My Lake.*

Other often overlooked places are *Susy-Q Creek, Goon Dip River, Chicken, Ripsnorter Creek, Old Grouch Top,* and *Bilge Creek.*

Arizona

"The Grand Canyon State"

True Facts and Silly Stats

Population: 3,677,985 (including 106,025 non-elderly)
Area: 113,510 sq. mi.
Capital: Phoenix
State Tree: Cactus
State Flower: Cactus
Principal Crop: Cactus
State Mineral: Particulate Quartz (Sand)
State Motto: We're Not California
Famous Person: Barry Goldwater
Most Famous Historical Event: Gunfight at the OK Corral
Principal Tourist Attraction: The Grand Canyon

Outrageous Tour Highlights

Visit Arizona, the garden spot of the Southwest. The natives proudly boast that their land is more lush than an asphalt highway. With much the same sense of humor that made the Vikings name a frozen island Greenland, Arizonans have named a town *Many Farms*. Today, Arizona is the popular destination of millions of tourists each year. In fact, tourism is one of the state's leading industries. The reasons for the state's popularity among travelers remain a mystery to many natives, including the folks of *Why*.

The warm dry climate of Arizona has long been known for its healthful qualities. The amazing weather of the state lures tourists from across the nation. The healthful climate is best

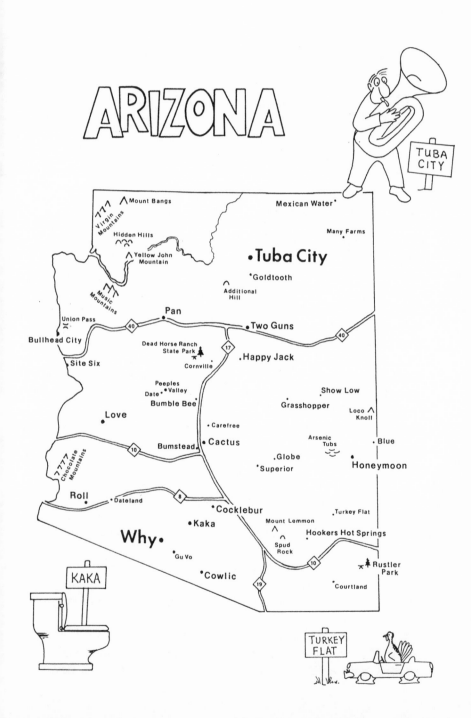

ARIZONA

TUBA CITY

Mount Bangs

Virgin Mountains

Hidden Hills

Yellow John Mountain

Mexican Water

Many Farms

•Tuba City

•Goldtooth

Additional Hill

Music Mountains

Union Pass

Pan

Two Guns

Bullhead City

40

40

Site Six

Dead Horse Ranch State Park

17

•Happy Jack

Cornville

Peeples Valley

Date•

Bumble Bee

Show Low

Grasshopper

Loco Knoll

Love

•Carefree

Bumstead

•Cactus

Arsenic Tubs

•Blue

10

•Globe

•Superior

Honeymoon

Chocolate Mountains

Roll

•Dateland

8

•Cocklebur

Turkey Flat

•Kaka

Mount Lemmon

Hookers Hot Springs

Why•

Spud Rock

Gu Vo

10

Rustler Park

•Cowlic

19

Courtland

KAKA

TURKEY FLAT

experienced by driving across the state on Interstate 40. During the summer, on this route, you can fry in *Pan.*

Arizona is popular among retirees. Some seniors move to Arizona permanently, others simply come for the winter months. An especially popular locale among seniors is *Cocklebur,* south of Interstate 8, near Casa Grande. Newcomers say the people in *Cactus* are stuck up, but attachments are easy to form in *Cocklebur.*

It is a little known fact that Arizona is popular with felons. This is easy to understand by visiting *Superior* on Highway 60, in the southeast portion of the state. See the *Superior* jail with *Superior* criminals who have appeared before the *Superior* Superior Court. Although there is no doubt that *Superior* is a popular judicial center, most criminals prefer to be captured at *Carefree* by the *Carefree* Police and spend their time in the *Carefree* Jail. Cow thieves prefer to do their heisting at *Rustler Park.* A visit to any of these locales beats going to *Courtland,* a town founded by a wagon train of pioneering lawyers.

Little needs to be said about dining out in Arizona. Southwestern cuisine is world famous and Arizona offers a veritable cornucopia of culinary delights. A brief visit to *Mount Lemmon* will give you a year's requirement of vitamin C. We recommend that you visit wondrous *Spud Rock* but avoid the potato dinner specials in the local restaurant. And a sure antidote for traveler's constipation is a visit to *Mexican Water.*

In terms of entertainment, Arizona has something for everyone. Enjoy the fine professional theatrical tradition at *Cornville.* Revel in easy listening at *Music Mountains.* For those who like to blow their own horn there is *Tuba City.* Take a tour of *Turkey Flat* and buzz by *Bumble Bee.* This excursion will inform you about both the birds and the bees. Visitors who enjoy dancing can hop into *Grasshopper.* The annual dance there is reputedly known as the Grasshopper hop. When you tire of sightseeing and feel in the mood for stimulating conversation, head for *Bullhead City.*

Arizona is a mecca for those in search of romance. It is easy to find *Love* in Arizona. *Love* is located on Highway 60, in La

Paz County between Salome and Wenden. Once you are there, relish the way it feels to be in *Love*. *Honeymoon* is another favorite destination of Arizona love tours. Some prim travelers to Arizona have noted that *Mount Bangs* is incongruously situated near the *Virgin Mountains*. A winter highlight of the Arizona romance tour is a warming dip in *Hookers Hot Springs*. Watch out for base flashers at *Show Low*. In Arizona, anyone can get to *Date*. *Date* is conveniently located near *Peeples Valley* just off Highway 89.

Other unusual and often overlooked places to see are *Additional Hill, Loco Knoll, Happy Jack, Arsenic Tubs, Gu Vo, Kaka,* and the *Chocolate Mountains*.

Arkansas

"The Toad Suck State"

True Facts and Silly Stats

Population: 2,362,239 (250 of whom are unrelated)
Area: 52,082 sq. mi.
Capital: Little Rock
State Motto: Regnat Populus (The People Rule)
State Flower: Apple Blossom
State Tree: Pine
State Sport: Spitting Tobacco
State Goal: One Shoe for Every Foot
Major Crime: Poaching
Annual Per Capita Income: $2,000 (or $3,500 with still)
Leading Architectural Style: Early American Outhouse
Most Important Person: Hillary Rodham Clinton
Major Tourist Attraction: Ozark Mountains

Outrageous Tour Highlights

Arkansas is one of the great states for outdoor recreational fun, be it hunting, fishing, hiking, or canoeing. Vast areas of rolling forested hills cover much of the north and west of the state. Delightful, clear, spring-fed rivers wind their ways through the countryside providing some of the most enjoyable canoeing in the United States. Like Texas, Arkansas was a southern state that served as a gateway to the west. At one time the Oklahoma Territory was administered from Fort Smith, Arkansas. The historical buildings, jail, and gallows in Fort Smith represent one of the most striking tourist attractions that survive from the days of the Wild West.

ARKANSAS

TOAD SUCK

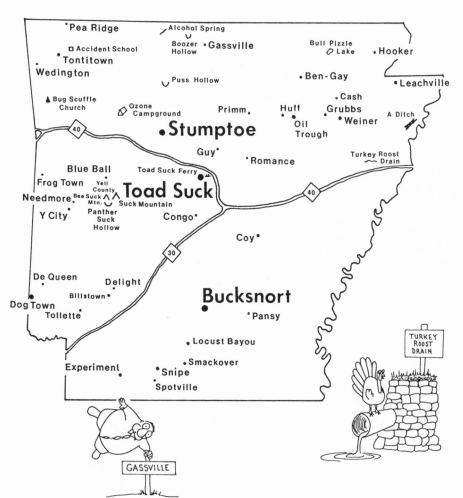

- Pea Ridge
- Alcohol Spring
- Boozer Hollow
- Gassville
- Bull Pizzle Lake
- Hooker
- Accident School
- Tontitown
- Wedington
- Puss Hollow
- Ben-Gay
- Leachville
- Bug Scuffle Church
- Ozone Campground
- Primm
- Huff
- Cash
- Grubbs
- Weiner
- A Ditch

Stumptoe

- Oil Trough
- Guy
- Romance
- Turkey Roost Drain
- Blue Ball
- Toad Suck Ferry
- Frog Town
- Yell County
- Needmore
- Bee Suck Mtn.
- Suck Mountain

Toad Suck

- Y City
- Panther Suck Hollow
- Congo
- Coy
- De Queen
- Delight

Bucksnort

- Billstown
- Dog Town
- Tollette
- Pansy
- Locust Bayou
- Experiment
- Smackover
- Snipe
- Spotville

GASSVILLE

TURKEY ROOST DRAIN

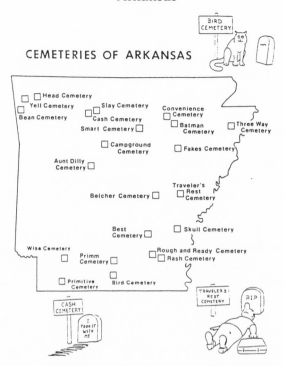

CEMETERIES OF ARKANSAS

To enjoy Arkansas, you need to enjoy the out-of-doors. Arkansas is a state that is justly famous for its camping delights. Pitch a tent and enjoy the atmosphere of *Ozone Campground* in the Ozark National Forest. Hunters can stop in *Snipe* in the southern protion of the state, where guides are available for world-famous Snipe hunts.

Outdoor vactioners will discover Arkansas' "sucks." Insist on visiting the extraordinary community of *Toad Suck* near Conway. Be certain not to miss the exciting yearly *"Toad Suck Daze."* Go on to have more extraordinary experiences at nearby *Toad Suck* Ferry. Three more "sucks" are west of *Toad Suck,* there is *Panther Suck Hollow, Bee Suck Mountain,* and just plain *Suck Mountain.*

One of the least known categories of outdoor attractions in Arkansas is its cemeteries. Why tour the cemeteries of New Orleans when Arkansas has the gamut from the *Primitive Cemetery* to the *Best Cemetery?* Visit *Traveler's Rest Cemetery* in the east central portion of the state. However, we cannot guarantee the accommodations. Or you can pitch your tents among the tombstones at *Campground Cemetery* north of Little Rock. If you are in the northeast visit a graveyard named after a famous superhero, *Batman Cemetery*. Can people be buried dead, alive, or inbetween, at *Three Way Cemetery*, southwest of *Blytheville*? People pretending to be dead are accommodated at *Fakes Cemetery*, but *Rough and Ready Cemetery* takes all comers.

The outdoor activity that goes on in Arkansas creates big appetites. Sample the height of Arkansas cooking at *Wiener* southwest of Jonesboro. Nowhere is the fine cuisine and dining ambiance better typified than at *Smackover* in southern Arkansas. For the best in southern fried foods, the true connoisseur must pay a visit to the fine restaurants of *Oil Trough* on Highway 14, west of Newport. The effects of the state's fast food emporiums can be noticed in *Gassville*, on Highways 62/412 west of Mountain Home. Outdoor adventurers can drown their troubles at *Alcohol Spring* and *Boozer Hollow* northwest of *Gassville*. And if you plan on doing any hiking near Walnut Ridge, in the northeast portion of the state, you may want to think twice before you quench your thirst at *Bull Pizzle Lake*.

The fresh air and outdoor exercise will undoubtedly strengthen the traveler's libido. Anyone can find *Romance* north of Little Rock. Male tourists can go northeast from *Romance* via *Cash* to *Hooker*, in the northeast corner of the state. Female tourists can go northwest from *Romance* to find *Guy* on Highway 16. Romantic tours of Arkansas usually end in *Delight* on Highway 26, west of Arkadelphia.

Tourists in need of repentance can visit *Bug Scuffle Church* near *Strickler* in northwestern Arkansas. It is one of the truly unique pilgrimage sites in North America.

Exhausted travelers will enjoy a soothing end to their Arkansas vacation at *Ben-Gay* near Poughkeepsie.

Other unusual places to see are *Pea Ridge, Turkey Roost Drain, Accident School,* and *A Ditch*.

California

"The Rough and Ready State"

True Facts and Silly Stats

Population: 29,839,250 (and some odd people)
Area: 156,297 sq. mi.
Capital: Sacramento
Topography: Shaky
State Tree: Redwood
State Flower: Marijuana
State Cloud: Smog
State Bird: Loon
State Motto: We Are Out of Therapy and Off Medication
State Spectacle: Hollywood Boulevard
State Food: Tofu
Famous Persons: Ronald Reagan, Richard Nixon
Major Tourist Attractions: Yosemite Valley, Lake Tahoe, and
    Sequoia National Forest

Outrageous Tour Highlights

It is believed that California was named after an earthly
paradise in a sixteenth century Spanish story. Over the years,
this earthly paradise has been the destination of immigrants and
travelers from all over the world. Today, it is the most populous
state in the United States. As a cultural melting pot, California
has come to tolerate a variety of different viewpoints. You can
experience such a different slant on life by visiting the California
town of *Incline. Incline* is located near the west entrance to
Yosemite National Park.

Many travel consultants recommend that the place to start

19

CALIFORNIA

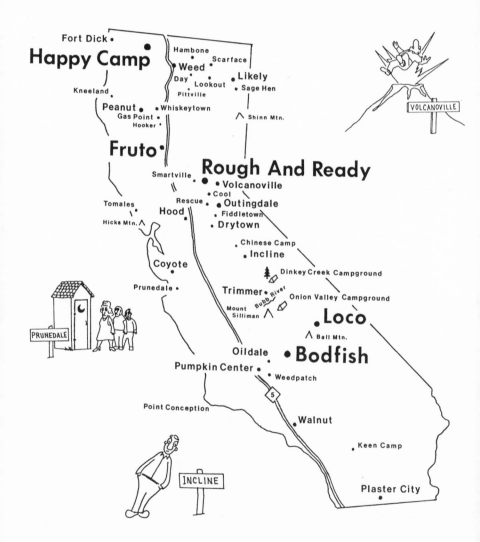

Fort Dick •

Happy Camp •

Hambone • Scarface
• **Weed**
Day Lookout • **Likely**
Pittville • Sage Hen

Kneeland •

Peanut • • Whiskeytown
Gas Point •
Hooker •

Fruto •

VOLCANOVILLE

Smartville • • **Rough And Ready**
• **Volcanoville**
• Cool
Tomales • Rescue • **Outingdale**
Hood • Fiddletown
Hicks Mtn. ∧ • **Drytown**

Shinn Mtn.

• Chinese Camp
• **Incline**

Coyote •

Dinkey Creek Campground

Prunedale • **Trimmer** • Bubb River • Onion Valley Campground
Mount
Silliman

Loco

PRUNEDALE

∧ Ball Mtn.

Oildale • • **Bodfish**
Pumpkin Center • • Weedpatch

5

Point Conception

• **Walnut**

• Keen Camp

INCLINE

Plaster City

a tour of California is at *Lookout* in Modoc county. Surpisingly, *Lookout* is located in northern California while Mount Whitney, the highest point in the 48 conterminous states, is located in southern California. This unfortunate positioning of *Lookout* means you won't be able to look out over much of California from *Lookout*. However, if you look to the west you may be able to see *Day*. An especially popular *Lookout* activity is watching *Day* lights at night. Not far from *Lookout* is the town of *Likely*. Strangers in *Likely* are known as the unlikely.

Geographically, California can be thought of as a human body. There is *Shinn Mountain,* near Highway 395, where you can go to get your kicks. East of Eureka is *Kneeland,* which is an interesting joint. And not too far up is *Fort Dick.*

The heart of California is located just off Highway 20, between *Smartville* and *Grass Valley.* This colorful place is *Rough and Ready*—a must stop for outrageous tourists. If you are rough, you can go on to *Hood* near Sacramento. If you are ready, you can go on to *Hooker* or *Ball Mountain.*

California offers many camping opportunities. Oriental tourists are especially welcomed at *Chinese Camp.* You will enjoy the close camaraderie you experience while fishing at *Dinkey Creek.* Not far away is the only river in the world named after a truck driver, scenic *Bubb River.* The best camping facilities in California are at *Keen Camp* not far from Palm Springs.

Californians are regarded as the most health-conscious Americans. This awareness may be based on California's agricultural richness. California produces a greater variety of crops and produce than any other state. To partake of this bounty, visit *Fruto* west of I-5, in Glenn County. From *Fruto* you can continue your health tour by heading north to *Peanut,* or south to *Prunedale.* Some travelers mistakenly believe that *Prunedale,* with only 1,500 people, will not have accommodations or activities for travelers. However, a visit to *Prunedale* will convince you that it is a regular resort town.

Always tolerant of different lifestyles, California still allows smoking outdoors. Smoke all you want at *Volcanoville,* but you are advised to avoid the eruptions at the local bars. Smokers are also advised to be careful of the cigarettes they are offered in the town of *Weed.*

California's educational system is the envy of the nation. Universities such as Stanford and the University of California at Berkeley are known worldwide. Educational opportunities at other, lesser known, California colleges and universities abound. The University of California at *Fiddletown* specializes in educating violinists. The SAT score entrance requirements are particularly high at the University of California—Smartville. Serious party animals flock to the State Universities at *Loco* and *Cool.* Smartaleck graduates of *Wiskeytown* Junior College finish their four-year degrees at *Plaster City* State University.

All good things must come to an end. Many California tours conclude the visit to paradise with a tearful farewell party in *Hambone.*

Other often overlooked places to visit are *Pumpkin Center, Onion Valley Campground, Point Conception,* and *Mount Silliman.*

Colorado

"The Hygiene State"

True Facts and Silly Stats

Population: 3,307,912
Area: 103,598 sq. mi. (more if you count the ups and downs)
Capital: Denver
State Flower: Rocky Mountain Columbine
State Bird: Lark Bunting
State Sport: Skiing
State Injury: Broken Leg
Leading Natural Resource: Tourists
State Motto: There Is More Gold in Tourists Than in Mining Claims
Highway for the Sober Only: US-550, Ouray to Durango
Major Tourist Attraction: Rocky Mountain National Park

Outrageous Tour Highlights

Colorado is one of the most popular tourist destinations in the United States. The spectacular Rocky Mountains offer beautiful vistas in the summer and excellent skiing in the winter. Denver, the largest city in the region, contains a number of interesting museums. The awesome Black Canyon of the Gunnison is one of the most remarkably sheer canyons in the world. The San Juan Skyway in southwestern Colorado offers extraordinary views of mountain ranges. Mesa Verde National Park, also in the southwestern part of the state, contains splendid Anasazi ruins, built by ancient native Americans.

Colorado also has a number of outrageous attractions that the unconventional tourist will not want to miss. Visitors can get all wrapped up in the vacation wonderland of *Mummy Range*. If

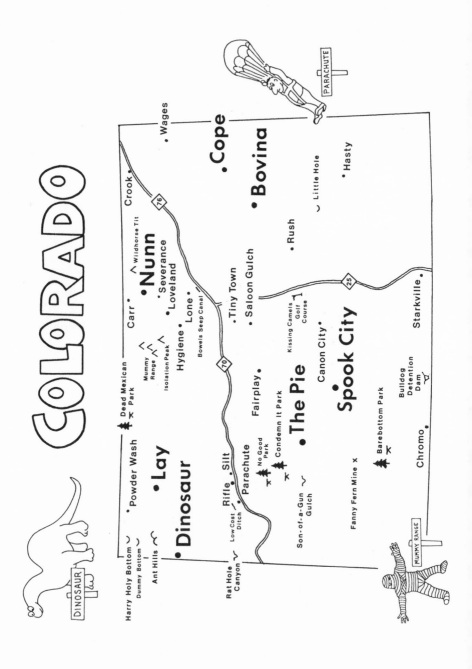

you want to get a bang out of your vacation go to *Rifle*, and if you want to have a bigger blast go to *Canon City*. Or you could put new excitement and variety into your love life at *Kissing Camels Golf Course* at Colorado Springs.

Vacationers leading a harried life can get away from it all at *Isolation Peak*. If that is not enough solitude, there is the town of *Lone* and if that's still not enough, there is always *Nunn*. If you want to drop out of the rat race, there is *Parachute*.

The town of *Hygiene* is famous for being all washed up, but it is still a nice place to visit. *Hygiene* was founded in 1850 by a wagon train of compulsively clean pioneers, who sought to tidy up the West and clean out the Indians. The founders of *Hygiene* were not happy living in *Silt*. Nevertheless, *Silt* was settled. The founders of *Hygiene* would not have enjoyed the crystal clear waters of *Bowels Seep Canal*.

We suggest that newcomers move to *Wages* and get a job with the city. Then you'll be working for *Wages*. If you work for the city of *Severance*, you'll get *Severance* pay.

Take a revealing visit to *Crook*, where you can meet the *Crook* mayor, the *Crook* sheriff, and the *Crook* Cub Scout leader. From *Crook* in the far northeast corner of Colorado, it's a long way to *Fairplay* in the center of the state.

Colorado is one state where you can get to *Lay* and be very far from *Loveland*. *Wildhorse Tit* was obviously named by very lonely miners. Such miners need to know how to get to *Cope*, on Highway 36.

Colorado contains some of the world's most remarkable parks. For the outrageous traveler, there is *Barebottom Park*, *Condemn It Park*, and *No Good Park*.

Colorado is not always what it is cracked up to be. This is particularly apparent at *Dummy Bottom*. *Fanny Fern Mine* is entertaining if you like to dig fanny ferns. Visit a most unusual religious shrine at *Harry Holy Bottom*.

Other often overlooked places are *Low Cost Ditch, Son-of-a-Gun Gulch, The Pie*, and *Bulldog Detention Dam*.

Connecticut

"Horse Heaven"

True Facts and Silly Stats

Population: 3,295,669
Area: 4,872 sq. mi.
Capital: Hartford
State Purpose: To Provide a place for New Yorkers to sleep
State Motto: We Do Not Pay New York Taxes
State Architectural Style: Latter Day Insurance Building School
State Flower: Mountain Laurel
State Bird: American Robin
State Fish: U.S.S. Nautilus
State Song: "Yankee Doodle"
State's Most Declined Industry: Whaling
Famous University: Yale
Major Tourist Attraction: Peabody Museum

Outrageous Tour Highlights

Connecticut is a small but densely populated New England state, where many of its citizens commute to work in New York City. Connecticut has been a model for other states, and the original charter of this state was a model for the United States Constitution. One of the first states to industrialize, Connecticut set the pattern for American manufacturing. Much of the early wealth of the state was based on the sea. The whaling and seafaring heritage of the area can be appreciated at the colorful and interesting historical site at Mystic Seaport.

This quintessential Yankee State has interesting place-names that suggest a variety of vacation possibilities. In fact,

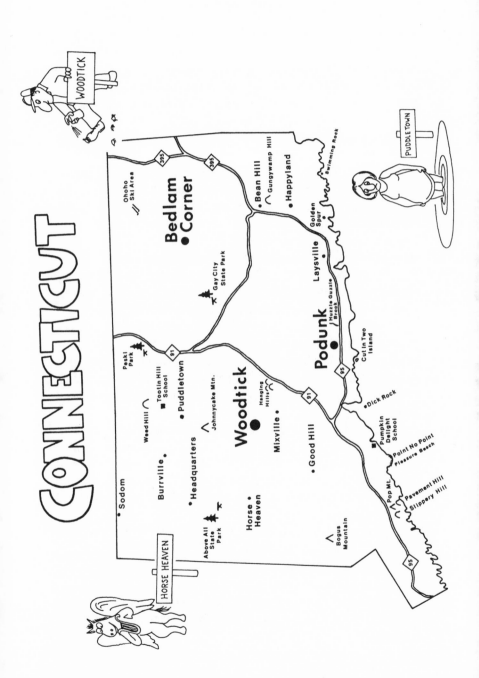

you can make your vacation headquarters in Connecticut at *Headquarters,* east of Mohawk Mountain State Park. From *Headquarters* you can travel south to experience *Horse Heaven* or north to party in *Sodom.* Other tourist spots in the area range from good to the sublime. Connoisseurs of hills will enjoy *Good Hill,* on local route 188. Visitors in search of more elevating experiences can visit *Above All State Park,* on scenic Highway 45. A slick place to visit is *Slippery Hill,* near Westport. City dwellers who dislike all the vegetation that covers rural hills in most states will feel at home visiting *Pavement Hill,* near *Pop Mountain,* in southwestern Connecticut. Contrary to its name, *Pop Mountain* is not a volcano. The pleasant ambiance of Connecticut is best experienced in *Happyland,* south of Norwich, and *Gay City State Park* east of Hartford.

After experiencing a Connecticut vacation, a visitor may not want to vacation anywhere else. This is particularly true for visitors who develop attachments in *Burrville* and *Woodtick.*

Intellectuals are attracted to Connecticut by its famous museums and universities such as Yale and the Peabody Museum. Visitors can ponder existential reality at *Point No Point* in Connecticut. Remarkable educational experiences are available for youngsters at *Tootin Hill School* and *Pumpkin Delight School.*

Although a visitor can experience *Horse Heaven* in Connecticut, there are a few places in the state to avoid. One is *Bogus Mountain.* And, there is the unfortunate case of *Cut in Two Island. Cut in Two Island* is appreciated only by those who think two is better than one. The visitor will not find peace and quiet in *Bedlam Corner.*

Finally, one may discover that the people of the state are quite class conscious. In Connecticut, if you don't amount to a hill of beans, you can't go to *Bean Hill.* On the other hand, the yachting set does not fit in at *Puddletown.*

Swimming Rock, Hanging Hills, Gungywamp Hill, Peski Park, and *Huzzie Guzzie Brook* are other unusual places to visit.

Delaware

"A State With Guts"

True Facts and Silly Stats

Population: 668,696
Area: 1,933 sq. mi.
Capital: Dover
Geographic Status: Second Smallest State
State Bird: Blue Hen Chicken
State Tree: Bonsai (so they would have room for a forest)
State Garden: Flower Pot
State Motto: We Have No Sales Tax
State Fiber: Nylon
Famous Family: du Pont
Place in History: First state to ratify the Constitution in 1787
Major Tourist Attraction: New Castle

Outrageous Tour Highlights

If you are searching for a vacation that takes guts, Delaware is for you. An outrageous tour of Delaware reveals *Broad Gut, Joes Gut, Indian Gut, Wire Gut, Old Womans Gut, Crooked Gut,* and *Quarter Gut,* to name a few. The *Hub* of Delaware is only a short distance from Head of the Gut. The term "gut" refers to a small waterway or creek. However, the original settlement of Delaware by European colonists did take "guts." The first Dutch settlement near today's Lewes was wiped out by Indians. An ancestral preoccupation with guts may explain why tiny Delaware's two regiments were among the best in the Revolutionary army. The people of Delaware are also known for sticking their necks out. This may explain why Delaware was the

29

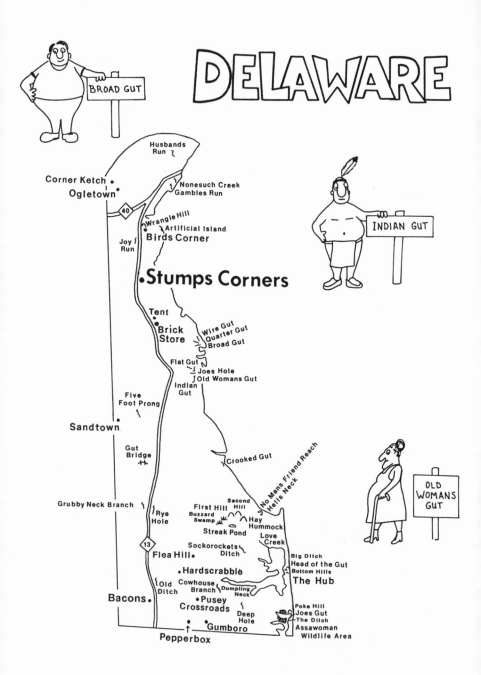

DELAWARE

BROAD GUT

INDIAN GUT

OLD WOMANS GUT

Husbands Run
Corner Ketch
Ogletown
Nonesuch Creek
Gambles Run
40
Wrangle Hill
Artificial Island
Joy Run
Birds Corner
Stumps Corners
Tent
Brick Store
Wire Gut
Quarter Gut
Broad Gut
Flat Gut
Joes Hole
Old Womans Gut
Indian Gut
Five Foot Prong
Sandtown
Gut Bridge
Crooked Gut
No Mans Friend Reach
Hells Neck
Grubby Neck Branch
Rye Hole
First Hill
Buzzard Swamp
Second Hill
Hay Hummock
Streak Pond
Love Creek
Sockorockets Ditch
Flea Hill
Big Ditch
Head of the Gut
Bottom Hills
Hardscrabble
The Hub
Old Ditch
Cowhouse Branch
Dumpling Neck
Bacons
Pusey Crossroads
Deep Hole
Poke Hill
Joes Gut
The Ditch
Assawoman
Wildlife Area
Gumboro
Pepperbox

first state to ratify a new document called a "Constitution." However, the habit of sticking one's neck out is not a pretty sight at the place called *Grubby Neck Branch*.

Few travelers realize when planning a vacation that Delaware is a shopper's paradise. Enjoy a wonderful shopping experience at *Brick Store*. Be sure to buy one of the charming brick key chains guaranteed never to get lost in a lady's handbag. Pick up one of the T-shirts with a famous brick blazoned across it. *Brick Store* is conveniently located just off Highway 13, in the north central region of the state. This is also the site of the first store in the famous failed retail chain, *Bricks-R-Us*. After you've seen *Brick Store*, try nearby *Tent*. If you feel the itch to escape other shoppers, drive south to *Flea Hill*.

Delaware is not only a primary supplier of chemicals and explosives to the U.S. government, but a proud participant in the history of U.S. space exploration. Delaware is the home of the nation's only landfill for space debris, *Sockorockets Ditch*. Not far away is another little known landmark, *Old Ditch*, the oldest known ditch in the original thirteen colonies. Archaeologists have found evidence that *Old Ditch* predates new ditches. If you feel size is more impressive than age, visit *Big Ditch* north of *The Hub*. If your vacation time is limited, visit a generic depression, *The Ditch* in the southeastern portion of the state. A tour of depressed localities in Delaware is not complete without a stop at *Deep Hole* between *Gumboro* and *Dumpling Neck*.

For those who would like to run the Delaware libido lap, you can pant through *Pusey Crossroads* and *Ogletown* to stare in awe at *Five Foot Prong*. An unsolved mystery is why Ogletown is situated at the opposite end of the state from *Streak Pond*.

Other unusual, often overlooked places are *Artificial Island*, *Nonesuch Creek*, *Poke Hill*, *Bottom Hills*, and *Stumps Corners*.

Florida

"America's El Dorado"

True Facts and Silly Stats

Population: 13,003,362 plus Cuba
Area: 54,157 sq. mi.
Capital: Tallahassee
State Flower: Orange Blossom
State Tree: Hurricane Flattened Palm
State Motto: Alligators on the Beach, Sharks in the Sea
State Bird: Plastic Flamingo
State Mineral: Calcium from shells
Major Tourist Attraction: Walt Disney World
Most Feared Disaster: Mickey Mouse Eaten by Alligators
Space Port: Kennedy Space Center

Outrageous Tour Highlights

The Spanish explorer Juan Ponce de Leon heard from natives of the New World about a land called "Bimini" which legend said had waters with miraculous curative powers and great wealth. This became Ponce de Leon's great quest, to find fabulous Bimini. On March 27, 1513, he found land which he named "Florida" (Land of Flowers). The term "Florida," like the term El Dorado, came to be synonymous with a place of wealth. He searched the countryside for treasure until the Indians, annoyed by his forays, wounded him fatally in 1521. Eventually it became apparent to the colonial authorities that Florida was not an island.

Today, the "wealth of Florida" is brought by tourists

FLORIDA

BRATT

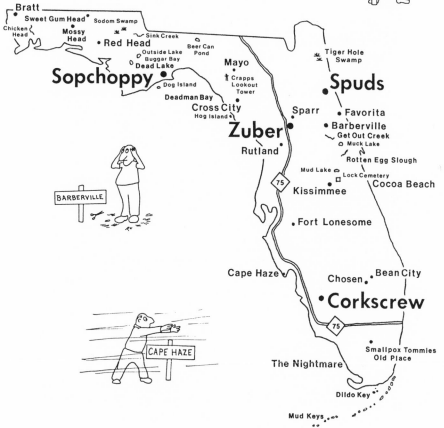

Bratt

Sweet Gum Head

Sodom Swamp

Chicken Head

Mossy Head

Sink Creek

Red Head

Outside Lake

Beer Can Pond

Buggar Bay

Dead Lake

Mayo

Sopchoppy

Crapps Lookout Tower

Dog Island

Deadman Bay

Cross City

Hog Island

Zuber

Rutland

Tiger Hole Swamp

Spuds

Sparr

Favorita

Barberville

Get Out Creek

Muck Lake

Rotten Egg Slough

Mud Lake

Lock Cemetery

Cocoa Beach

75

Kissimmee

Fort Lonesome

Cape Haze

Chosen

Bean City

Corkscrew

75

Smallpox Tommies Old Place

The Nightmare

Dildo Key

Mud Keys

BARBERVILLE

CAPE HAZE

searching for beaches, sunshine, and fun. Services and tourism are Florida's major industries. Visitors spend 26 billion dollars a year in the state. Most visitors come to enjoy themselves in famous places like Miami, Orlando, Fort Lauderdale, and Key West. But Florida also has a wealth of outrageous places, away from the crowds. Let's be adventurous and explore Florida's alternative tourist haunts.

A favorite vacation spot is *Favorita* in the northeastern portion of the state. *Favorita* is just north of Daytona Beach on Highway 1. Although *Favorita* is a favorite, many people choose *Chosen* near Belle Glade in the southern half of the state. *Chosen* may be popular because the specialty restaurants of *Bean City* are only a few minutes' drive away. *Favorita* is less conveniently located in relation to the gourmet restaurants of *Spuds*.

Florida has a warm temperate climate north of Orlando and a subtropical climate to the south. Those who prefer the warm temperate climate can take the biblical nature tour of *Sodom Swamp* in Northern Florida. Those who prefer a subtropical climate can put an extra twist on their vacation at *Corkscrew*.

While you are visiting southern Florida, be sure to take in the Keys. Among the least visited islands in the key chain are *Dildo* and *Mud Keys*. To avoid Miami Beach crowds, head west to *Smallpox Tommies Old Place*. You may want to bring plenty of aspirin and be prepared to stay at least two weeks. A little known vacation experience in Florida is *The Nightmare*. *The Nightmare* vacation of your life can be had near *Shark Point* on the west side of Everglades National Park.

A popular activity in Florida is experiencing the crystal clear waters of natural springs. Glass bottom boat tours are a major tourist attraction. The most famous springs are Wakulla Springs near Tallahassee, and Silver Springs near Ocala. If you prefer not to wait in line or have other boats mar your view, take the glass bottom boat rides at *Muck Lake, Rotten Egg Slough,* or *Beer Can Pond* near Miccosukee. You would be amazed how well you can see beer cans in crystal clear water. A contest is held daily, and the visitor correctly guessing the number of beer cans wins an all expense paid visit to *Buggar Bay.*

An unusual body of water in Florida is Outside Lake. This suggests the other lakes in Florida are inside.

Many people visit Everglades National Park in order to see wildlife. Other animal watching opportunities are available in Florida. Domestic animal refuges are found on *Dog* and *Hog Islands.* *Tiger Hole Swamp,* near Jacksonville, is for those who enjoy watching tiger holes.

Perhaps, like Ponce de Leon, you want to look for treasure in Florida. An easy way to begin your search is to scan the countryside from *Crapps Lookout Tower,* located in the northern portion of the state.

Other often overlooked places to visit are *Chicken Head, Sweet Gum Head, Red Head,* and *Get Out Creek.*

Georgia

"The Peach State"

True Facts and Silly Stats

Population: 6,508,419
Area: 58,060 sq. mi.
Capital: Atlanta
Largest City: Atlanta
State Motto: A Yankee Tourist Is Easier to Pick Than a Bale of Cotton
State Food: Cracker
State Citizen: Cracker
State Pyromaniac: General Sherman
Famous Book: *Gone With the Wind*
Famous Politician: Jimmy Carter
Famous Musicians: Ray Charles, Otis Redding, James Brown, and Little Richard
Major Historic Site: Savannah
Major Tourist Attraction: Chattahoochee National Forest

Outrageous Tour Highlights

Georgia is one of the largest and most dynamic southern states. Energetic Atlanta is Georgia's political capital and its economic powerhouse. Atlanta is historically famous for being burned by General Sherman during the Civil War. Atlanta is also famous as the home of civil rights activist Martin Luther King, Jr. Margaret Mitchell, who wrote *Gone With the Wind,* also lived in Atlanta. Savannah preserves a fine historic district that will charm tourists. The Okefenokee Swamp is in southern

GEORGIA

BIBB COUNTY

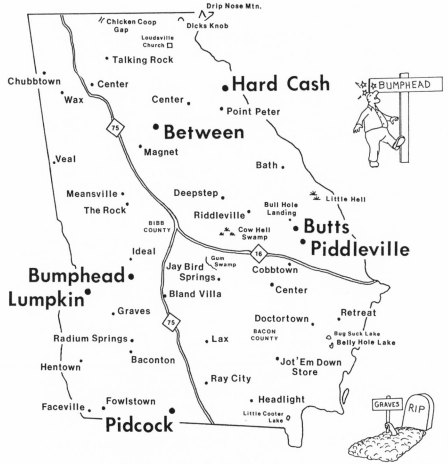

Drip Nose Mtn.

Chicken Coop Gap

Dicks Knob

Loudsville Church

Talking Rock

Chubbtown

Center

Wax

Center

Hard Cash

BUMPHEAD

Point Peter

75

Between

Magnet

Veal

Bath

Meansville

Deepstep

Little Hell

The Rock

Riddleville

Bull Hole Landing

BIBB COUNTY

Cow Hell Swamp

Butts

Ideal

Gum Swamp

16

Piddleville

Bumphead

Jay Bird Springs

Cobbtown

Lumpkin

Bland Villa

Center

Graves

Doctortown

Retreat

75

BACON COUNTY

Radium Springs

Lax

Bug Suck Lake

Belly Hole Lake

Hentown

Baconton

Jot'Em Down Store

Ray City

Faceville

Fowlstown

Headlight

GRAVES   RIP

Pidcock

Little Cooter Lake

Georgia and rivals the swamps of Florida and Louisiana with its vast wildlife resources.

Georgia is an outrageous vacationer's paradise. Delightfully different, Georgia offers an infinite variety of things to do. Brighten your day at *Headlight*, or get on the beam at *Ray City*. A visit to *Radium Springs* will leave you with a warm glowing feeling. If such brilliant attractions aren't what you're looking for, we're sure you will be drawn to *Magnet*, east of Interstate 75.

For a slick tourist attraction visit *Wax*. A number of fine journalists work on the *Wax* paper. Things get a bit sticky at *Wax* during the summer. But things are sticky all year around at *Gum Swamp*.

Visit *Ideal*, Georgia, on Highway 90, for a truly *Ideal* vacation. About forty miles south of *Ideal* is *Bland Villa*. *Bland Villa* parties are reputed to be miraculous cures for insomnia. Georgia offers more stimulation at *Lax*, where you can watch *Lax* men and *Lax* women cavort. They have a *Lax* minister who isn't even a television evangelist. Incidentally, the ex-citizens of *Lax* are known as the ex-*Lax*.

The best place to enjoy Halloween is the town of *Graves*. The scariest time is when people leave town and are seen emerging from *Graves*. Except for Halloween, things usually seem pretty dead in *Graves*.

Sometimes Northerners have a difficult time finding their way around Georgia. Georgia has three *Centers*, none of which are in the center of the state. Two *Centers* are in the northern part of the state, and one *Center* is in the southern part of the state. Fortunately for travelers, the town of *Between* is actually between *Centers*. *Between* is on Highway 10, east of Atlanta. (Although you may find yourself feeling comfortable and snug in *Between*, don't get jobs in that town, because then you'll be in *Between* jobs.) Trying to find your way around Georgia's *Centers* and in *Between* may lead you to *Riddleville*.

If you get lost in Georgia, asking for directions is not always helpful because the natives are renowned as taciturn folk with heavy accents. Visitors have said that even stones are more talkative. This is evidenced by *Talking Rock.* Georgia's pioneers noticed this rock's chatter and were quick to differentiate *Talking Rock* from *The Rock,* which apparently did not engage in verbal discourse. The founding of *Loudsville Church* northeast of Talking Rock may have been an attempt to have sermons heard over the talking.

When you visit Georgia, take a walking tour of the streets of *Deepstep* or *Bumphead,* and learn why the state has a *Doctortown.* Physicians in *Doctortown* advise that you take a big hanky with you when you visit *Drip Nose Mountain.* When bad weather threatens, leave *Drip Nose Mountain* before you are caught in a big blow.

Other colorful places to visit are *Cow Hell Swamp, Belly Hole Lake, Little Cooter Lake, Dicks Knob,* and *Jot 'Em Down Store,* and *Bull Hole Landing.*

Hawaii

"The Aloha State"

True Facts and Silly Stats

Population: 1,115,274 plus Japan
Area: 6,427 sq. mi. (less at high tide)
Capital: Honolulu
Original State Name: Sandwich Islands
State Flower: Yellow Hibiscus
State Mineral: Lava
State Tree: High-rise Hotel
Major Industry: Tourism
State Dance: Hula
State Endangered Species: Native Hawaiians
State Fish: Mainland Sucker
Famous Person: King Kamehameha
Major Tourist Attractions: Waikiki Beach and Hawaii Volcanoes
     National Park

Outrageous Tour Highlights

The number one vacation destination of most American tourists is fabulous Hawaii. With 750 miles of tropical coastline, few places offer as many opportunities for surfing, swimming, or just relaxing on a beach. With over 900 species of native plants, visitors can stroll through gardens such as the Hilo and Hawaii Tropical Gardens, or hike along rugged nature trails in Kokee State Park. A visit to Waimea Canyon on the island of Kauai offers the traveler a view of the "Grand Canyon of the Pacific."

The native Hawaiians who settled the Islands, perhaps as early as AD 300, named most topographic features in their own

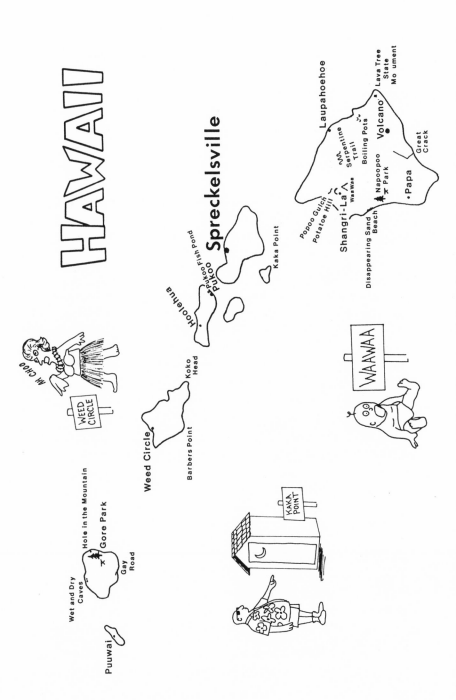

language. Therefore, this tropical paradise offers limited out-rageous tour possibilities for English speakers. Nevertheless, let's begin our tour of the former "Sandwich Islands" on the island of Kauai.

Kauai There are several different botanical zones on the island of Kauai because of variations in rainfall, temperature, wind, and barometric pressure. Accommodations for visitors on Kauai are equally varied. You can stay at luxury hotels in *Princeville,* or if you are budget conscious, you can seek less formal accommodations at *Wet and Dry Caves. Wet and Dry Caves* offer you a choice of dwellings with or without water. Prices for lodging can be high on Kauai, but don't stay at some hole-in-the-wall, at least stay at *Hole-in-the-Mountain.*

Oahu, Molokai, Maui and Kahoolawe Next visit the island of Oahu for a stroll through beautiful *Weed Circle.* As you travel to the island of Molokai, test your fishing skills at *Pukoo Fish Pond.* On Maui, browse the native arts and crafts stores of *Spreckelsville.* Before heading to the big island of Hawaii, make a brief stop on Kahoolawe to take in the view from *KaKa Point.*

Hawaii "The Big Island" When you reach the "Big Island" make the community of *Volcano,* which bubbles over with warmth, your tour headquarters. *Volcano* is an inland location not far from the coast. Once you are settled at *Volcano,* set aside a day for a leisurely tour of the island. This can be done by following a scenic loop. First, drive west from *Volcano* through *Great Crack* to visit *Papa.* After visiting *Papa,* stop to see whether *Disappearing Sand Beach* is there, then go on to *Shangri-La,* and lunch at *Potato Hill.* Slither home in the afternoon via the *Serpentine Trail.* Cook your own supper at *Boiling Pots* near Hilo and then watch the sunset at *Lava Tree State Monument.*

Other unusual places to visit are *Popoo Gulch, Gore Park,* and *KoKo Head.*

Idaho

"The Humble State"

True Facts and Silly Stats

Population: 1,011,986
Area: 82,413 sq. mi.
Capital: Boise
State Bird: Bluebird
State Flower: Potato
State Fossil: Potatosaurus
State Road Kill: Mashed Potatoes
State Motto: Esto Potatus (It Is a Potato)
Most Famous Quote: "Give me potatoes, or give me death!"
Official State Outerwear: Potato Skins
First Tourists: Lewis and Clark
Famous Person: Sacagawea
Major Tourist Attractions: Sun Valley, Sawtooth National Recreation Area, River of No Return Wilderness Area

Outrageous Tour Highlights

Idaho is a magnificent state. It is so mountainous that you are rarely out of sight of a mountain when driving through the state. Some mountains, like the Sawtooth Range, north of Sun Valley, are as beautiful as the Grand Tetons in Wyoming. It is said that if Idaho were flattened out, it would be bigger than Texas.

Idaho is also a geological wonderland. There are numerous hot springs, volcanic cones, old lava flows, and lava caves. Hells Canyon, along the western border between Lewiston and Weiser, is deeper than the Grand Canyon. The Snake River

43

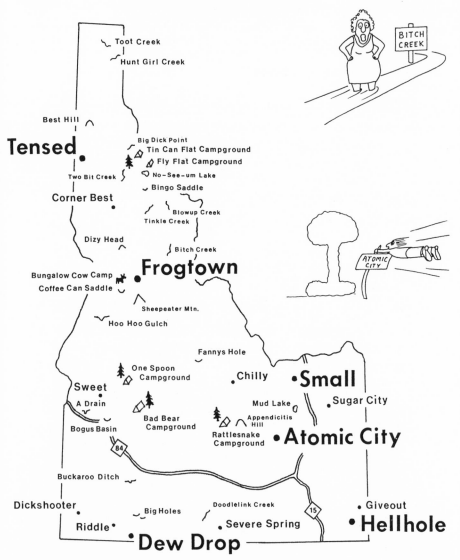

canyon between American Falls and Twin Falls has sections with sheer walls that weep with waterfalls in spring.

With all this grandeur, one would think Idahoans would be a proud people who would brag like Texans and Alaskans. Instead, they are very humble and assume that no matter where a visitor is from, it is probably a better place than Idaho. Even a visitor from the Black Hole of Calcutta is likely to hear the phrase, "This is probably not much compared to where you're from."

In terms of colorful place-names, Idaho is one of the best in the U.S. Names like *Pocatello, Chubbuck,* and *Blackfoot* are considered ordinary. With wind chills in winter reaching seventy degrees below zero, the Idahoan predilection for understatement is evidenced by the town of *Chilly.* Understanding for the frailty of life is indicated by *Giveout.* There are so many unusual place-names that after driving through the state, one easily comes to assume that the road sign "Frost Heaves Ahead" refers to a town.

There are different specialty tours of Idaho. The frontier heritage is still alive in the state. You can see cowboys herding cattle as you drive the byroads of the state. Vacationers will find many opportunities to experience a cowboy way of life in Idaho. Begin a cowboy's tour of the state by viewing *Buckaroo Ditch* not far from Bruneau in the southwest portion of the state. Then head north on Highway 95 to Riggins. Not far away is *Bungalow Cow Camp* which offers the finest amenities in cowboy camping. And, for a real eye-opener, experience morning coffee on the range at *Coffee Can Saddle.*

The fresh mountain air will help you work up a hearty appetite. Fortunately *Sheepeater Mountain* is nearby, where you can have a filling meal of mutton. Then head north to the Clearwater National Forest area, where you can learn about cowboys' favorite recreational activity and how they do it at *Bingo Saddle.*

Frontier Idaho was a place where men were men, and women were in short supply. This may explain the existence of *Hunt Girl Creek* in Idaho. But women on the frontier learned how to take care of themselves, and male travelers are advised not to offend Idaho women at *Dickshooter.*

Idaho offers many great camping possibilites. In central Idaho, you may have to share your tent with an unexpected visitor at *Bad Bear Campground.* Get a buzz out of *Rattlesnake Campground* on the Middle Fork of the Payette River. Experience the unusual dining restrictions at *One Spoon Campground* near *Crouch.* In the northeast, you can pitch your tent on level terrain at the popular *Tin Can Flat Campground* near Avery. In case of overflow crowds, there is nearby *Fly Flat Campground.* Experience the vastness of the Old West at *Small.* There are primitive restroom facilities at *Tinkle Creek.* You can also enjoy the water sport of navigating your boat on *No-See-um Lake.* Or, have a toot at *Toot Creek.*

Last but not least, there is the popular "hole" tour of Idaho. Tourists who are impressed by size can go to *Big Holes* in the southwestern portion of the state. Those who have a devilish bent should visit *Hellhole* near Montpelier in southeastern Idaho. And travelers with other interests can head for *Fannys Hole* near Challis.

Other unusual, often overlooked places to see are *Doodlelink Creek, Big Dick Point, Blowup Creek, Appendicitis Hill, Atomic City, Two Bit Creek,* and *Hoo Hoo Gulch.*

Illinois

"Land of Lincoln"

True Facts and Silly Stats

Population: 11,466,682
Area: 55,646 sq. mi.
Capital: Springfield
Largest City: Chicago
State Motto: This Is the Land of Lincoln, We Never Heard of Al
    Capone
State Flower: Violet
State Tree: White Oak
State Bird: Stool Pigeon
Most Famous Politician: Abraham Lincoln
Most Noted Crime Fighter: Elliot Ness
World's Tallest Skyscraper: Sears Tower
Most Spectacular View: Lake Shore Drive, Chicago
Major Tourist Attraction: Cahokia Mounds State Historic Site

Outrageous Tour Highlights

The state of Illinois is dominated by the metropolitan area
of Chicago. Lake Shore Drive gives the best view of the
impressive and spectacular Chicago skyline. The Sears Tower is
the tallest skyscraper in the world. Chicago is also graced with
fine cultural attractions such as the Art Institute of Chicago,
Fields Museum of Natural History, the Museum of Science and
Industry, and Shedd Aquarium. A variety of famous people
have lived in the state, including Jack Benny, Frank Lloyd
Wright, Wild Bill Hickok, and the infamous Al Capone.

Illinois is justly famous for the spectacular figures who have

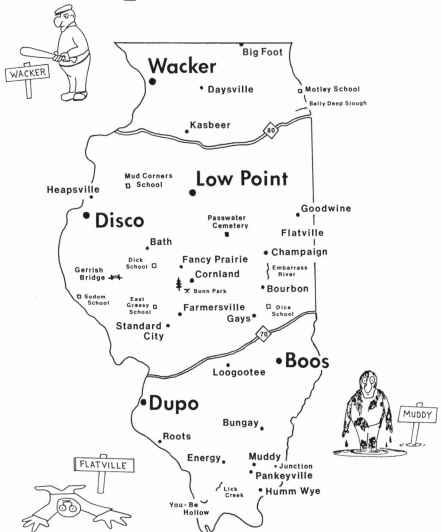

ILLINOIS

WACKER

Wacker

Big Foot

• Daysville

Motley School

Belly Deep Slough

• Kasbeer

80

Mud Corners
School

Low Point

Heapsville

Goodwine

Disco

Passwater
Cemetery

Flatville

• Bath

• Champaign

Dick
School

Fancy Prairie

Embarrass
River

Gerrish
Bridge

Cornland

Sodom
School

Bunn Park

• Bourbon

East
Greasy
School

Farmersville

Dice
School

Gays •

**Standard
City**

70

• Boos

Loogootee

• Dupo

MUDDY

Bungay •

• Roots

FLATVILLE

Energy •

Muddy

• Junction

Pankeyville

Lick
Creek

• Humm Wye

You - Be
Hollow

lived there. Abraham Lincoln is an example. The presence of *Big Foot* in Illinois, is less well known. *Big Foot* is on Highway 23, near the northern border of the state.

Illinois is a prairie state that consists almost entirely of flat to modestly rolling country. Despite being the sixth most populous state in the U. S., Illinois is a major agricultural state, usually second only to Iowa in corn production. The Illinois landscape has been a source of great intellectual inspiration. The place-names of the state reflect this inspired insight. We marvel at the creative minds that thought up the town names *Flatville* and *Junction*. Only people whose minds soar to flights of fantasy could have produced the names *Farmersville* and *Cornland*. The creator of the name *Fancy Prairie* was not worried about a contradiction of terms on the plain plains.

Standard City was named by people who thought that if you've seen one town, you've seen them all. This town has it all, *Standard City* lunatics, *Standard City* politicians, *Standard City* delinquents, and *Standard City* problems. *Standard City* is the generic choice for visitors who only have time to see one Illinois city.

Education has made Illinois what it is. The state's school system has managed to combine size with specialized instruction. *Greasy* kids are educated at *East Greasy School*. The muddy children go to *Mud Corners School*. Almost anybody can go to *Motley School,* where they fit right in with the *Motley School* students. Would-be gamblers can attend *Dice School,* which brings new meaning to the term "attendance roll." There is also a *Dick School* and *Sodom School*. Whatever their names might suggest, their curricula is not X-rated.

Since the Roaring Twenties, Chicago has been famous for speakeasies, bars, and drinking. Today, "Sports bars" are especially numerous and popular in Chicago. But you can find many other good places to drink in Illinois. You can enjoy *Goodwine, Champaign,* and *Bourbon* in the state. At *Kasbeer,* on Highway 26, you can find out what "kas" is, and how the locals ferment it. Drinking is not a great art at *Lick Creek,* where the use of drinking glasses is bypassed. Perhaps because of a fondness for drinking, the only combination cemetery-restroom in the world can be found at *Passwater Cemetery.*

For cheap, dirty thrills there is nothing like a trip to *Muddy.* *Muddy* is on Highway 45, in the southern part of the state. The people of Illinois do have a *Bath,* but it is a long way from *Muddy.* If your interests run to hanky-panky, you can get halfway there by stopping in *Pankeyville,* just south of *Muddy.*

A stop at *Wacker,* Illinois, is likely to leave you feeling beat, but you still have some distance to go before you can arrive at *Lowpoint.* After reaching *Lowpoint* on your Illinois vacation, you will need to visit *Energy,* west of Interstate 57. If you still need a rest, park your buns at *Bunn Park* in Springfield.

Other often overlooked places are *Bely Deep Slough, You-be-Hollow,* and *Gerrish Bridge.*

Indiana

"The Hoosier State"

True Facts and Silly Stats

Population: 5,564,228
Area: 35,936 sq. mi.
Capital: Indianapolis
State Motto: Don't Call Us Outer Chicago
State Tree: Tulip Poplar
State Song: "On the Banks of the Wabash, Far Away"
Major Event: Indianapolis 500 Car Race
Famous Person: Michael Jackson
Best Known Speller: J. Danforth Quayle
Best Known Criminal: John Dillinger
Famous Football Team: The Fighting Irish of Notre Dame
State Fantasy: To be a football player in a race car
Major Tourist Attraction: Indiana Dunes National Lakeshore

Outrageous Tour Highlights

The state motto of Indiana is "Crossroads of America."
The city of Indianapolis, at the heart of the state, is a hub of
transportation. Four Interstate Highways intersect in Indianapolis, making the city a strategic location for industry and
commerce. Indianapolis is also home of the famous car race, the
Indianapolis 500.

Perhaps one of the most famous unusual place-names in
American history is from Indiana. This is *Tippecanoe*. William
Henry Harrison, leading the militia, won a battle against the
Shawnee Indians at the *Tippecanoe River,* (near today's
Lafayette) in 1811. The victory became known as the *Battle of
Tippecanoe,* and may have been a major factor in Harrison's

election as the ninth president of the United States. The battlefield is commemorated as a State Historic Site.

Indiana has other unusual place-names that have not been recognized in history books. For example, there is *Hogs Defeat Creek*, where a battle was apparently won against swine. There is *Tumblebug Creek* where no known battle was won. Near the *Tippecanoe Historic Site* is the town of *Battle Ground*, whose community events have never been quiet or boring. *Shirkieville* and *Loafers Station* were apparently settled by people who wanted to avoid stress.

A variety of vacation experiences can be found at outrageous Indiana places. Have a slick time in *Petroleum* on Highway 1. Twist the night away at *Cyclone* or *Disko*. Golfers will surely want to reach *Parr*, west of Interstate 65, in northeastern Indiana. In southern Indiana, watch the old guy try to climb *Scudder Hill*. This can be marginally more entertaining than visiting *Weedpatch Hill* during the allergy season. Find out what turns Bennett on at *Bennetts Switch*, near Kokomo.

Visitors will find a wide variety of dining possibilities in Indiana. Enjoy the restaurant fare at *Gnaw Bone*. An interesting insight into the state's concept of food service hygiene can be gained at *Lick Fork State Recreation Area*. It is even more amazing that this is considered a form of state recreation. Or visit the *Burns City* restaurants. And finally *Aroma*.

Indiana's concern for those who have gone before can be seen in cemetery names. Experience passion beyond the grave at *Horney Cemetery*. Plant your pickle at *Pickle Cemetery*. Relax in your posthumous retirement at *Idle Cemetery*.

Finally, no visitor to this fine state should miss the much acclaimed *Hot Lick Creek*.

Other unusual, often overlooked places are *Stink Ditch*, *Hasty Ditch*, *Popcorn*, and *Growcock Branch*.

Iowa

"The Manly and Fertile State"

True Facts and Silly Stats

Population: 2,787,424
Area: 55,965 sq. mi.
Capital: Des Moines
State Industry: Pork Production
State Avocation: Pork Consumption
Political Agenda: Getting Pork
State Festival: Pork Festival
State Flower: Pigweed
State Mineral: Dirt
Famous Person: John Wayne
Most Popular Activity: Bingo
Major Tourist Attraction: Effigy Mounds National Monument

Outrageous Tour Highlights

Iowa is a land of rich black soil between two great rivers, the Mississippi and the Missouri. The rich soil is considered the finest in America. While the state of Iowa ranks 29th in size in the U.S., it produces one tenth of the nation's food supply. Iowa has also been the nation's leading pork producing state. The gentle terrain, ideal for agriculture, is usually not considered a tourist magnet. However, don't assume that because of Iowa's prairie, agricultural base, it is a dull state. You'll find more things to see and do in Iowa than you ever imagined. "Discover Iowa's treasures."

Discerning travelers begin their outrageous tour of Iowa by first visiting the north central region of the state. This is an area

54

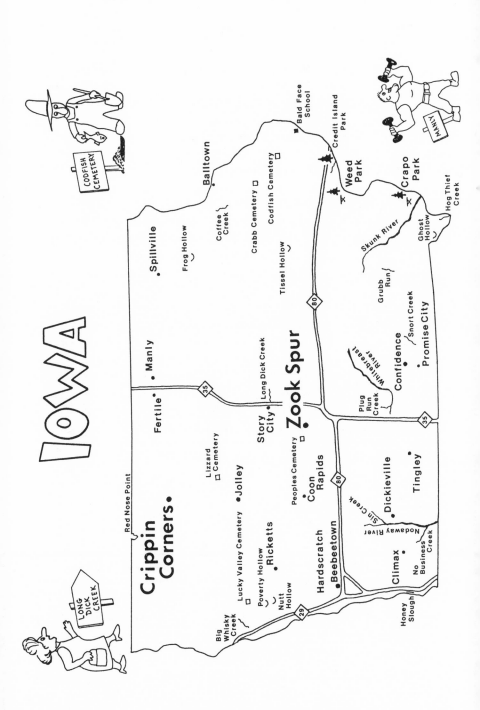

that was flattened by ancient glaciers. Here, awesome views of a featureless landscape lead to unbridled passions. The traveler will discover that the town of *Fertile* is situated near the town of *Manly*. If a *Manly* man married a *Fertile* woman, the couple could drive east to honeymoon at *Balltown*.

The romantic tour of Iowa continues by driving to the southwestern portion of the state. If you make *Tingley* by the early part of the day, you can easily go on to *Dickieville* south of *Sin Creek*. From there, it's only a short distance to *Climax*.

Savor Iowa's respect for the environment. No nuclear wastes are buried here. However, virtually anything else is buried in the state. In the eastern part of the state are *Crabb Cemetery* and *Codfish Cemetery*. In the north central part of the state is *Lizzard Cemetery*. So unusual are the burial practices, that one cemetery has been labeled the *People's Cemetery* to indicate that people rather than crabs, codfish, or lizzards are buried there. The presence of a *Lucky Valley Cemetery* suggests that "Lucky" may be a misnomer.

The waters of Iowa are justly famous and a "must stop" for tourists. In the western part of the state, there is *Big Whiskey Creek* and in the north there is *Red Nose Point*. Travelers who have a deep thirst can drive southeast to *Snort Creek*. Too much exuberant intoxication can be remedied by a sobering stop at *Coffee Creek*.

Those looking for *Promise* and *Confidence* will find both in the central part of southern Iowa. If you seek sophisticated, urbane delights, don't be put off by Iowa's reputation for "American gothic." Take in the ambiance of *Frog Hollow*. Revel in the prosperity of *Hardscratch Township*. View a natural wonder at *Long Dick Creek*. And, gain insight into the corridors of power by watching the big shots in *Beebeetown*.

Conclude your tour by going east to the Mississippi River. There you can enjoy nature in the parks of Iowa. Stare spellbound at the floral extravagance of *Weed Park* in Muscatine. Venture deep into areas few have trod in Burlington's

Crapo Park. From there, you may bid fond adieu to the outrageous Hawkeye State.

Some other unusual, often overlooked places are *Crippin Corners, Zook Spur, Plug Run Creek, No Business Creek,* and *Bald Face School.*

Kansas

"The Sunflower State"

True Facts and Silly Stats

Population: 2,485,600
Area: 81,783 sq. mi.
Capital: Topeka
State Motto: Noli in Publico Illam Facere (Don't Do It In Public)
State Flower: Sunflower
State Tree: Windmill
State Song: "Home on the Range"
Source of Topographic Relief: Cow Pies
Famous Lawmen: Wyatt Earp, Bat Masterson
Famous Politician: Dwight Eisenhower
Famous Medical Pioneer: Goat Gland Brinkley
Major Industry: Selling gas to people going to Colorado
Major Tourist Attraction: Dodge City Frontier Town and Boot
    Hill

Outrageous Tour Highlights

Kansas is famous for three different historic events. First, it was a state traversed by the Santa Fe and Oregon Trails. Second, it was the site of pre-Civil War conflict between abolitionists and pro-slavery forces. And third, it is famous as the wild and woolly cowtown heartland of the Old West. All of these events left their mark on Kansas places. During the pre-Civil War era, settlers from the North and South flocked to the Kansas Territory to sway the determination of whether it would be a free or slave state. For a time, Kansas had two capitals. One was the "Northerner's" capital in Topeka and the other was the "Southerner's" capital in Lecompton. The strain of these events

58

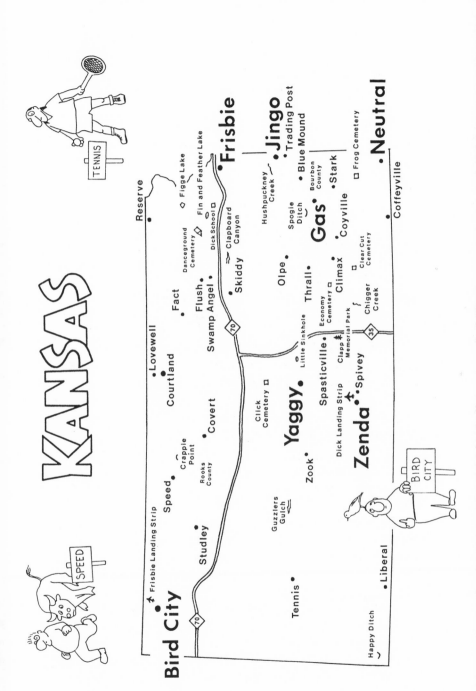

may have been too much for the state's founders, because Kansas has one of the most peculiar collections of place-names in North America.

A tour of Kansas towns reveals *Yaggy, Jingo, Frisbie,* and *Olpe.* A tour of Kansas waterways reveals *Chigger Creek, Spogie Ditch, Happy Ditch, Hushpuckney Creek,* and *Figge Lake.* Other features include *Clapboard Canyon* and *Crappie Point.*

If you plan on flying to Kansas, you may want to consider arriving at *Frisbie Landing Strip* to avoid the more hectic transportation hubs.

Some Kansas towns have been immortalized in literature. Among these is *Zenda. Zenda* lies southeast of *Zook,* and not far from *Spivey* on Highway 42. A convict in the local jail is, of course, the inspiration for the famous novel and movie *The Prisoner of Zenda.*

The town of *Spasticville* lies between Wichita and Newton. Members of the Spasticville marching band have been waiting patiently to show their stuff in the Rose Bowl Parade.

The town of *Tennis* can be found in western Kansas near *Friend* on Highway 83. If you get a traffic ticket in *Tennis,* you will have to make an appearance before the *Tennis* court. However, while you are in town, be sure to purchase footwear at the *Tennis* shoe store. The annual town dance is known as the *Tennis* ball. Watch out for confidence men in the town because you don't want to be the victim of a *Tennis* racket.

For an automotive romp through Kansas cruise into *Speed* or *Skiddy.* Idle in *Neutral,* then head over to *Gas,* east of Iola on Highway 54. By the way, those who just drive by are guilty of passing *Gas.* Later you can immerse yourself in *Bourbon County* or *Guzzlers Gulch.*

Conclude your tour of Kansas by driving through *Bird City* on Highway 36. Observe the quaint hand gestures of the natives as they bid you farewell.

Other unusual, often overlooked places you shouldn't miss are *Little Sinkhole* and *Swamp Angel.*

Kentucky

"The Lick State"

True Facts and Silly Stats

Population: 3,698,969
Area: 39,674 sq. mi.
Capital: Frankfort
Largest City: Louisville
State Motto: It's Better to Have a Fast Horse, Than a Fast Woman
State Bird: Fried Chicken
State Drink: Bourbon
State Plant: Bluegrass
State Music: Bluegrass
Famous Horse Race: Kentucky Derby
State Hero: Daniel Boone
Famous President: Abraham Lincoln
Major Tourist Attraction: Mammoth Cave National Park

Outrageous Tour Highlights

Kentucky is a border state that shows characteristics of both the North and South. It was the birth place of both the rival leaders of the Civil War, Abraham Lincoln and Jefferson Davis. There is a wealth of beautiful scenery in this state. Daniel Boone National Forest and Natural Bridges Resort Park in eastern Kentucky are visitor favorites. Another major tourist destination is Mammoth Cave south of Louisville. The Bluegrass Downs are the center of Thoroughbred racing in the United States. With all of these attractions, no one can lick Kentucky as a vacation spot. And a look at Kentucky place-names reveals that Kentuckians can lick about anything.

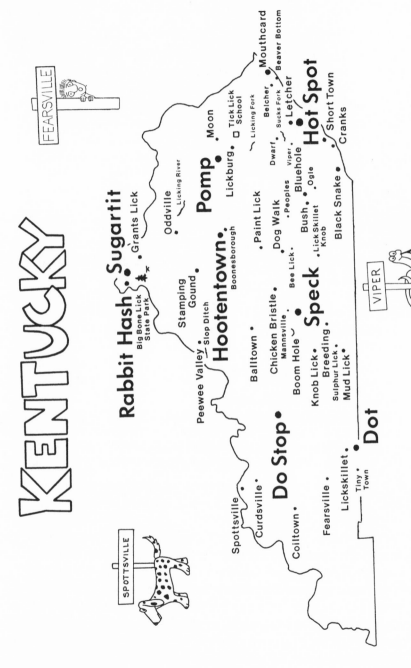

A predilection for licking is clearly evident at *Paint Lick* on Highway 52, east of Danville. Participation in a *Paint Lick* festival can be a mind-altering experience. After visiting this colorful Kentucky community, head southwest to *Knob Lick,* and south to *Sulphur Lick* and *Mud Lick.* Learn about one of the great tongues in American History at *Grants Lick.* Animal lovers enjoy *Bee Lick* and *Tick Lick School.*

Louisville, Kentucky, is a popular center of entertainment and nightlife. Many travelers enjoy the bars and live music along Bardstown Road and Baxter Avenue in Louisville. But Kentucky has other great entertainment opportunities. Thrill to the throbbing excitement of *Hot Spot,* Kentucky. *Hot Spot* is ironically located near *Letcher,* in the southeastern portion of the state. Then have a hoot in *Hootentown,* near *Boonesborough.*

Kentucky is well known for delicious foods. Colonel Harlan Sanders opened his first restaurant featuring Kentucky fried chicken in Corbin, Kentucky, in 1940. Restaurants featuring his recipe are now found all over the world.

If you are seeking culinary treats, don't limit yourself to Kentucky's famous places. The state has other places that will tickle your palate. You can sink your teeth into an unusual dairy treat at *Curdsville,* just off the Audubon Parkway in western Kentucky. Be sure to dine in elegance on the state's favorite food at *Rabbit Hash,* southwest of Covington. Gourmet travel "musts" are *Lickskillet, Lick Skillet Knob,* and *Big Bone Lick State Park.* Some visitors are so taken by Kentucky cuisine that they go beyond *Licking Fork* to *Sucks Fork.* After a gourmet tour of Kentucky, relax at *Belcher.*

If you are looking for an out of this world vacation, take a trip to *Moon.* You can do a *Moon* trip in Kentucky much cheaper by car than NASA can by rocket. *Moon* is located on Highway 172, in the eastern potion of the state. Here, you can meet *Moon* men, *Moon* women, and *Moon* children.

Texans and Alaskans brag about the sizes of everything in their states, but Kentuckians value the petite. Visit *Short Town* and discover their love of the small. If *Short Town* is too much, there is *Dwarf.* The people from *Dwarf* vacation in *Peewee Valley.* If you are looking for a smaller resort community, there is *Tiny Town,* at the junction of Highways 79 and 41. For even less, visit *Speck.*

Only brave tourists should visit *Fearsville,* Kentucky. If you are cold-blooded enough, you can unwind at *Black Snake.* Labor relations are a deadly affair when they strike in *Viper. Coiltown,* Kentucky, is for those who want to stay wound up.

Learn unusual theories about the world at *Cranks.* If *Cranks* does not provide you with strange enough experiences, there is always *Oddville.* You will undoubtedly be cheered by a stay in *Bluehole,* Kentucky. Find out what makes chickens mad at *Chicken Bristle,* near Hustonville. Attempts to control cockroaches in a local motel led to a town being named *Stamping Ground.* Finally, visit *Ogle,* Kentucky, and cast your eyes toward *Sugartit.* But for the modest, there is *Do Stop.*

Other often overlooked places are *Slop Ditch, Dog Walk,* and *Boom Hole.*

Louisiana

"The Dry Prong State"

True Facts and Silly Stats

Population: 4,238,216
Area: 44,520 sq. mi.
Capital: Baton Rouge
Largest City: New Orleans
State Motto: Is That an Alligator Shoe, or Is a Gator Swallowing
    Your Foot?
State Tree: Cypress
State Flower: Magnolia
State Song: "Give Me Louisiana"
State Coin: the French Quarter
State Pirate: Jean Lafitte
State Crustacean: Crawfish
State Food: Gumbo
State Mud: Gumbo
State Music: Jazz
Major Tourist Attraction: Mardi Gras

Outrageous Tour Highlights

Louisiana is a distinctive slice of Americana made from a blend of French, Anglo-American, and African cultures. The cultural and economic center of the state is New Orleans. The French Quarter of New Orleans is the most famous tourist attraction in the state. Jazz musicians, historic buildings, and a joyous party atmosphere make the French Quarter an irresistible tourist attraction. New Orleans's sedate Garden District preserves a fine sample of 19th Century residential architecture.

65

LOUISIANA

FROGMORE

Trees
Oil City
Belcher
Corney Bayou
Log Cabin
Gassoway
Transylvania
Latex
Knot Point
Start
Quitman
Cooterville
Womble Break
Stinkfinger Creek
Extension
Mammy Jude Bayou
Waterproof
Dry Prong
Funny Louis Bayou
Big Cash Bayou
Frogmore
Many
Self Cemetey
Ball
Bayou de Sot
Whiskey Chitto
Meeker
Cravens
Bunkie
Elizabeth
Sugartown
Blanche
Batchelor
Mix
Fluker
Beggs
Bundick Creek
Port Barre
Bat
Duckroost
10

Happy Jack
Bayou Touch-me-not
Triumph
Bayou John Bop

TRANSYLVANIA

WATERPROOF

The great swamps of southern Louisiana provide a semi-tropical paradise for migrating water fowl. The swamps are filled with alligators, turtles, and birds to delight nature lovers. The Cajuns have thrived in these swampy areas and visitors enjoy encountering the distinctive Cajun culture. Colorful place-names are also a highlight of Louisiana. The state welcomes the traveler with a wealth of outrageous locations.

A particularly attractive aspect of spending a vacation in Louisiana is the price. Louisiana offers great accomodations, food, and entertainment at comparatively low cost. A good place to begin your Louisiana vacation is at *Start* east of Monroe. You can go to *Start* and stop, or if you have money continue touring. Keep a lot of cash on hand if you plan to visit *Big Cash Bayou* between *Waterproof* and *Frogmore*. An alternative for travelers on a budget is *Little Cash Bayou*. Visitors financing their vacation with a loan may find that *Extension* is a particularly attractive destination. *Extension* can be found on Route 562, in the northeastern portion of the state. Another economical place to stay is *Log Cabin* on Highway 425. Although the accommodations may be rustic, travelers who find *Log Cabin* too expensive, can spend the night in *Trees* or *Duckroost*. If *Trees* or *Duckroost* are too much for your pocketbook, you will need to go to *Beggs* which is located along Interstate 49.

Louisiana has the ultimate economical resting place for travelers who die during their vacation. Little expense is involved when you do it yourself at *Self Cemetery*.

Visitors can get great meals in New Orleans for as little as five dollars. You can also eat well for even less while touring the countryside. Most appreciated by tourists is the famous Cajun cooking. Other culinary treats are available in Louisiana. *Sugartown,* of course, is a real treat. Try *Oil City* cuisine or sample the remarkable food at nearby *Belcher*. Later travel to *Gassoway*.

In Louisiana, the traveler will encounter the use of French terms. For example, "petite" for little. Place-names can be abbreviated in local usage. This combination leads to the conversion of rather staid Petite Bliss (a waterway), to *Tit Bliss,* a place with a completely different connotation. No doubt, tourists would rather visit *Tit Bliss* than *Petite Bliss.* One would hate to speculate on the origin of *Bundick Creek* or *Funny Louis Bayou.*

Romantically inclined visitors can go to *Blanche* then on to *Ball,* but should avoid *Bayou Touch-me-not* and *Dry Prong.*

Other unusual places to see are *Bayou John Bop, Corney Bayou, Womble Break,* and *Mammy Jude Bayou.*

Maine

"The Peekaboo Mountain State"

True Facts and Silly Stats

Population: 1,233,223
Number of Seafood Restaurants: 1,500,348
Area: 30,995 sq. mi.
Capital: Augusta
Largest City: Portland
State Flower: White Pine Cone and Tassel
State Bird: Chickadee
State Crustacean: Lobster
State Motto: Lobsters and Tourists Both Mean Money, but You
    Don't Have to Talk to the Lobsters
Chief Agricultural Crop: Rocks
Famous Writer: Harriet Beecher Stowe
Major Tourist Attraction: Acadia National Park

Outrageous Tour Highlights

Although it is the largest in size of the New England states, Maine has a relatively small population. The result is an uncrowded state which draws numerous outdoor loving tourists. Thousands of lakes and rivers are found in Maine. Hunting, fishing, canoeing, and hiking are big attractions during the warmer seasons. Skiing is popular in the winter. The rugged coastline and its charming fishing villages are a major draw for tourists. This most famed Yankee state is best known for its lobster fisheries and for seafood in general.

The view that the citizens of this state are as cold, quiet, and flinty as Maine's mountains is surely an exaggeration. The

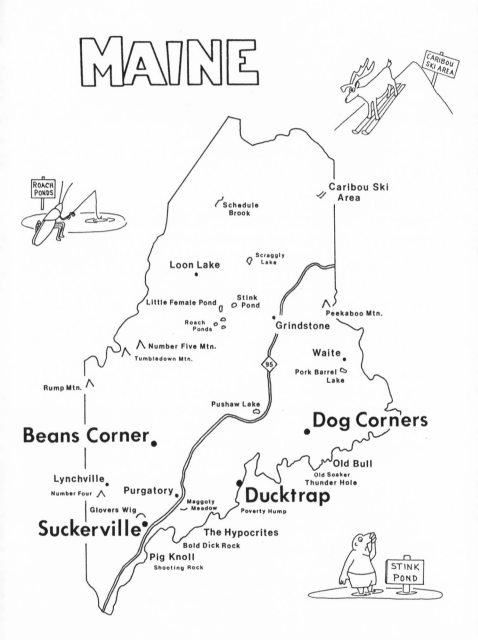

MAINE

ROACH PONDS

CARIBOU SKI AREA

Schedule Brook

Caribou Ski Area

Scraggly Lake

Loon Lake

Little Female Pond

Stink Pond

Roach Ponds

Grindstone

Peekaboo Mtn.

Number Five Mtn.

Tumbledown Mtn.

Waite

Pork Barrel Lake

Rump Mtn.

Pushaw Lake

95

Dog Corners

Beans Corner

Old Bull

Old Soaker Thunder Hole

Lynchville

Number Four

Purgatory

Ducktrap

Poverty Hump

Glovers Wig

Maggoty Meadow

Suckerville

The Hypocrites

Bold Dick Rock

Pig Knoll

Shooting Rock

STINK POND

place-names of the state paint another picture. Surely, *Rump Mountain* and *Bold Dick Rock* point to hidden depths in the state's character. Only the locals can tell you what goes on at *Peekaboo Mountain.*

Get away from that boring job and have the vacation of your life in Maine! But if you like the same old grind, visit *Grindstone.* Enjoy the most unusual fishing in North America at *Roach Ponds.* No unplanned stream use is allowed at *Schedule Brook.*

You don't have to die in Maine to go to *Purgatory. Purgatory* is near Interstate 95, east of Lewiston. After spending some time in *Purgatory,* indulge your worst instincts at *The Hypocrites,* south of East Boothbay. A visit to *Maggoty Meadow, Ducktrap,* or *Dog Corners* will make you feel as though you were in purgatory.

A bad economic situation has kept the state from maintaining its natural wonders. The most obvious example is *Tumbledown Mountain.* If the people of Maine allow this deterioration of their mountains to continue, the state will soon be as flat as Kansas. The shocking condition of *Stink Pond* and *Scraggly Lake* should serve as warning of what can happen, if you don't take care of a body of water. Times have also been tough at *Poverty Hump.* Maybe these sites are so deprived because places like *Pork Barrel Lake* and *Old Soaker* are hogging all of the funds. Last but not least, travelers who can't get to Congress can witness the next best thing and hear aged politicians make promises at *Old Bull.*

Other unusual, often overlooked places to visit are *Pig Knoll, Little Female Pond,* and *Number Five Mountain.*

Maryland

"A Place With Points"

True Facts and Silly Stats

Population: 4,798,622
Area: 9,838 sq. mi.
Capital: Annapolis
Largest City: Baltimore
State Motto: We Are Not Washington, D.C.
State Bird: Baltimore Oriole
State Tree: White Oak
State Crustacean: Soft-Shell Blue Crab
State Barber: Baltimore Clipper
Famous Athlete: Babe Ruth
Famous Writer: Upton Sinclair
Major Tourist Attraction: Baltimore Harborplace

Outrageous Tour Highlights

Maryland borders much of the extrordinarily rich marine estuary of Chesapeake Bay. This bay was famous in the past for its oyster beds, and is now noted for its delicious soft-shelled blue crabs. Baltimore is the dominant city in Maryland and was a famous port and ship building center in America's past. This maritime tradition can still be seen in Maryland at the U.S. Naval Academy at Annapolis.

Maryland, strategically placed on the eastern seaboard, beckons visitors with many remarkable points. Some of these are *Booby Point*, *Pagan Point*, and *Love Point*. All are located along Chesapeake Bay.

A popular Maryland destination is *Boring*, off Highway 30, in the northern portion of the state. It is not known how *Boring* could have been established southwest of *Spook Hill* because spooks are usually anything but boring. Nevertheless, visitors tour the *Boring* downtown and have fascinating conversations with the *Boring* residents.

Stimulating Maryland tours are also available of *Dulls Corner*, with optional day excursions to *Ordinary Point*. Other popular attractions in the state include the spectacular fireworks display in *Fizzelburg* and in avant-garde shops in *Funkstown*.

The people of Maryland love animals. This is apparent by the several places named for animals. There is *Frogtown*, *Dogtown*, and *Birdsville*. *Mousetown* is widely known for its fine cheeses. People who want to go ape will enjoy *Ape Hole Creek*.

Maryland is adjacent to the political activity of Washington, D.C. Here the product of the activity of the nation's greatest political minds can clearly be seen in *Crapo*. Each year national politicians gather at *Jesterville* to work out the federal budget. Great political commentaries are inspired by *Haha Branch*. Politicians rarely get to *Level*, although many claim residency at *Finksburg*. Most political business is done at *Deal Island*.

Safety should be the traveler's first concern when touring Maryland. Stay at *Guard* to avoid injury at *Accident* while on your way to *Breakneck Hill*. If you die in *Accident* and cannot afford to buy a plot, there is nearby *Lease Cemetery*.

Accommodations for the traveler in Maryland are unequaled. You can stay at quaint "bed and breakfast" inns that give you a hint of nineteenth century life, or you can stay at *Cavetown*, where accommodations provide guests with an even earlier form of quaint lodging.

The wonderful cuisine of Maryland is famous worldwide. They even have some tasty place-names like *Beantown*, *Bread and Cheese River*, and *Chewsville*.

The Maryland female ideal has been formed by a combination of the eastern career woman sophisticate and the cultivated southern Belle. You can run into this charming hybrid at *Dog and Bitch Islands*. The value Marylanders put on their womenfolk is indicated by *Dames Quarter*. Most women seek out *Love Point*. But those women seeking cheap thrills find their way to *Pagan Point* or *Manbone Island*. Both sexes search out *Layhill*.

Other often overlooked places are *Zippy Creek*, *Booze Creek*, *Ogle Junior High School*, *Cacaway Point*, *Point Look-In*, and *Glots*.

Massachusetts

"The Old Colony"

True Facts and Silly Stats

Population: 6,029,051
Area: 7,826 sq. mi.
Capital: Boston
State Motto: You're Doing What With That Tea?
State Bird: Chickadee
State Flower: Mayflower
State Fish: Cape Cod
Pilgrim Landing Zone: Plymouth Rock
State Witch Court: Salem
Famous Historic Event: Boston Tea Party
Famous Persons: Paul Revere, John Kennedy
Famous Writers: Longfellow, Thoreau, Emerson, Melville, Hawthorne, Alcott, Dickinson, Poe, and Whittier
Major Tourist Attractions: Cape Cod, Old North Church, and Walden Pond

Outrageous Tour Highlights

Massachusetts was founded by Puritans seeking to ensure the freedom of their religion. The largest city in the state is Boston which is historically associated with many of the epochal events leading to the Revolutionary War and the founding of the United States. The Freedom Trail through downtown Boston leads the tourist to numerous historical locations. Many charming and historic towns dot the countryside.

Despite the fact that Massachusetts earns over twelve billion dollars a year from out-of-state visitors, many tourists

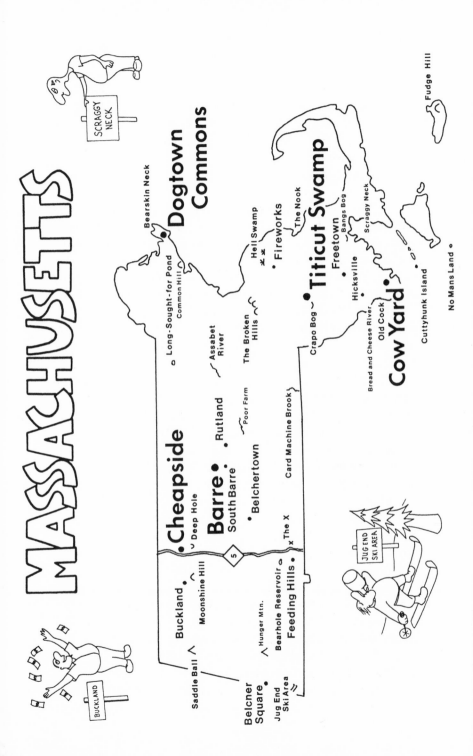

MASSACHUSETTS

SCRAGGY NECK

BUCKLAND

JUG END SKI AREA

Bearskin Neck

Dogtown Commons

Long-Sought-for Pond
Common Hill

Hell Swamp

The Nook

Fireworks

Titicut Swamp

Bangs Bog
Freetown
Scraggy Neck

Hicksville

Crapo Bog

Old Cock

Cow Yard

Bread and Cheese River

Cuttyhunk Island

No Mans Land

Fudge Hill

Cheapside

Deep Hole

Assabet River

The Broken Hills

Barre
South Barre

Rutland

Belchertown

Poor Farm

Card Machine Brook

Buckland
Moonshine Hill

Hunger Mtn.

Bearhole Reservoir
Feeding Hills

The X

Saddle Ball

Belcner Square

Jug End Ski Area

overlook the state. This may be due to the state's outrageous places. Visitors should not be put off by Massachusetts' *No Mans Land.* The name *No Mans Land* has been changed on some American maps to *Nomans Land.* This may be an attempt to make the place more appealing.

The fact that Massachusetts has *The Broken Hills* and *Common Hill* has not helped the tourist business. Who wants to drive to the outskirts of Boston to see *The Broken Hills,* or drive north to Marblehead to see the *Common Hill?* People who enjoy water sports and yachting have been frustrated by the fact that Massachusetts has a *Long Sought-For Pond.* Travelers who love to eat have been put off by Massachusetts' simple *Bread and Cheese River* and *Hunger Mountain* in the Berkshire Hills.

Known to the world as a nonviolent place, Massachusetts prides itself as a safe place to visit. It is difficult to convince out-of-state visitors of this fact, however, with places named *Cuttyhunk Island* and *Titicut Swamp.*

Despite places such as *Hell Swamp* and *Poor Farm,* Massachusetts actually has many exciting places to visit. A jug of wine and a pair of skis is all you need for adventure at *Jug End Ski Area.* A visit to *Deep Hole,* near Greenfield, provides a refreshing break from experiencing ordinary holes.

Massachusetts also offers numerous shopping opportunities. Look for bargains at *Cheapside.* Shop until you drop at *Freetown.* See how much you can get for a buck at *Buckland.*

Massachusetts offers many opportunities to get together and meet others. Travelers plagued with a spastic stomach can meet at *Belcher Square.* Those with a spastic colon can meet at *Crapo Bog.* Singles tired of "meat market" bars can pick up dates at the *Cow Yard* near New Bedford. Visitors can meet man's best friends at *Dogtown Commons.*

Massachusetts is known as a sexually tolerant state. No doubt, *The X* deserves its rating. You only need visit *Barre* to know this. If you prefer southern exposures, there is *South Barre.* Make love in the mud at *Bangs Bog* near Wareham. See astounding examples of mounted mounting at *Saddle Ball* north of Cheshire. And for women fond of antiques, there is *Old Cock* near Fall River.

Other unusual places to visit are *The Nook, Bearskin Neck, Scraggy Neck, Feeding Hills,* and *Bearhole Reservoir.*

Michigan

"The Free Soil State"

True Facts and Silly Stats

Population: 9,328,784
Area: 56,959 sq. mi.
Capital: Lansing
Largest City: Detroit
State Motto: Nobody Is Going to Buy Those Little Japanese
   Cars
State Flower: Apple Blossom
State Bird: Ford Thunderbird
State Animal: Mercury Cougar
Chief Industry: Auto Manufacture
Growth Industry: Unemployment Compensation
Leading Gallery: Detroit Institute of Art
Famous People: Henry Ford, Madonna, Magic Johnson, Tom
   Selleck, Pontiac, and Malcolm X
Major Tourist Attraction: Greenfield Village

Outrageous Tour Highlights

Michigan's abundant resources and location on major
shipping routes have made the state an industrial leader. But
Michigan is also a tourist magnet. Income from tourism com-
petes with income from auto manufacturing. Major tourist
destinations are Michigan's 3,200 miles of scenic lakeshore,
including Sleeping Bear Dunes National Lakeshore, Mackinac
Island, and Isle Royale National Park. Michigan has a wealth of
museums and festivals for the visitor. These include the Henry
Ford Museum and Greenfield Village, the Holland Tulip Festival,
and the National Cherry Festival in Traverse City. A look at

MICHIGAN

FREE SOIL

Two Hearted River

Worm Lake

Witch Lake

Dollar Settlement

Sugar Island

Neebish Island

Dafter

Helps

Gros Cap

Hog Island

Cross Village

Good Heart

Bliss

Poverty Island

75

Honor

Loud Dam
Foot Dam

LOUD DAM

Butman

Grind Stone City

Free Soil

Wooden Shoe Village

Tallman

Popple

Doc and Tom River

Crump

Bitely

Jam

Lum

Elsie

BITELY

Hell

Breedsville

Climax

Maybee

Hodunk

Cement City

Woodtick Peninsula

Michigan place-names also reveals that the state has a wealth of interesting locales overlooked in standard tour guides.

Michigan's place-names indicate that the state has a particularly fine citizenry. Nowhere is this more evident than at *Good Hart* on Lake Michigan. The only destination that can compare to visiting *Good Hart* is experiencing *Bliss* a few miles north. However, if a visitor feels one *Good Hart* in Michigan is not sufficient, one can cruise down *Two Hearted River* near Muskallonge Lake State Park on the Upper Peninsula.

Michigan has over eighteen million acres of forest. This vast expanse of forest can cause visitors from the prairie states to lose their sense of direction and to go into a state of shock known as "green panic." Be prepared and plan your travel needs carefully, because *Helps* is hard to find in Michigan. *Helps* is located northeast of Iron Mountain in the Upper Peninsula.

Many visitors to Sleeping Bear Dunes National Lakeshore are beguiled by views of Lake Michigan and assume distances are less than they actually are. Some visitors have set out in uncomfortable shoes on trails over the dunes, and assume the lake is only a short distance away. Instead, night falls, their feet give out, and they need to be rescued by helicopter. Visitors can avoid this problem by planning ahead. Throw away your street shoes and get a sturdier pair at *Wooden Shoe Village* west of I-75, before heading for *Sleeping Bear Dunes.* As anyone who has worn wooden shoes can tell you, no matter how short a distance may seem, you won't walk far from your car in wooden shoes.

There are other problems a visitor to Michigan may encounter. You may find that *Grind Stone City* can grate on you. You'll need to cover your ears at *Loud Dam* near Oscoda. It is best to humor the residents of *Cross Village,* as it is difficult to deal with *Cross Village* police. Visitors find they have a hard time being decisive in *Maybee* southwest of Detroit. Prom night lotharios take their chances in the *Maybee* motel. Tourists who are set in their ways prefer *Cement City* southeast of Jackson.

You can find *Honor* in Michigan on Highway 31, southwest of Traverse City. Interesting to note that when you are away from it, you are a person without *Honor*. If you can't find your way back, you have lost *Honor*.

Michigan offers many shopping opportunities. An outrageous consumer will want to stop by for a complimentary bag of dirt at *Free Soil*. You can also save money on your laundry bill at the *Free Soil* cleaners.

Other unusual places are *Dollar Settlement, Doc and Tom River,* and *Woodtick Peninsula*.

Minnesota

"The Gopher State"

True Facts and Silly Stats

Population: 4,387,029
Area: 79,548 sq. mi.
Capital: St. Paul
Largest City: Minneapolis
State Motto: Water Is for Waterskiing, Beer Is for Drinking
State Name Origin: Indian word meaning, "Where did all these Scandinavians come from?"
State Tree: Red Pine
State Song: "Hail Minnesota"
State Flower: Pink and White Lady's Slipper
Famous Writer: F. Scott Fitzgerald
Famous Singer: Prince
State Expression: Uff-da
Major Tourist Attraction: Minnehaha Falls

Outrageous Tour Highlights

Minnesota is a land whose surface has been carved by ancient glaciers. The result is a land with little topographic relief and a vast number of lakes. These numerous sparkling lakes have made water recreation one of the main attractions of the state. Outdoor enthusiasts enjoy the great opportunities for fishing and canoeing. Waterskiing was invented in Minnesota. Minnesota's principal urban area is composed of the twin cities of Minneapolis and St. Paul which are famous for a high quality of life. St. Paul used to be named Pig's Eye. As the early name

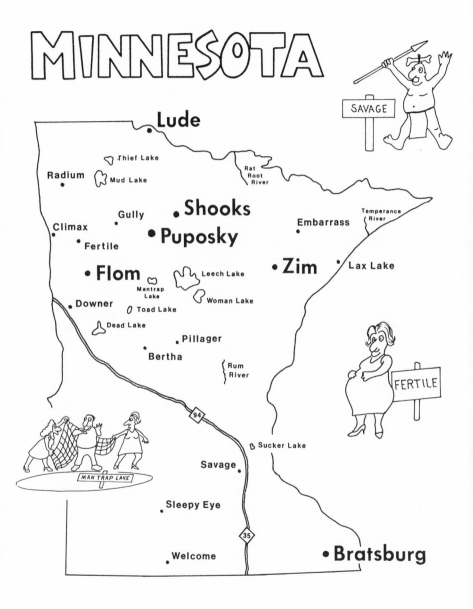

for St. Paul suggests, Minnesota has a variety of alternative destinations for the tourist seeking outrageous places.

Minnesota is famous for its remarkable lakes. What visitors could resist dipping their toes into wondrous *Leech Lake*. Take the whole family and enjoy the crystal clear waters of *Mud Lake*. The *Mantrap Lake* is a mecca for single women. *Woman Lake* is obviously for the men. You can discover true vacation peace at *Dead Lake*. Or meet the beautiful people at *Toad Lake*.

Although Minnesota is known for its scenery, there is also the malcontents' tour of the state starting with *Bratsberg* in the southeast. This is followed by a stop at *Savage* to attend a *Savage* festival or sports event and then on to *Pillager* and ends at *Thief Lake*, where travel funds tend to disappear.

The visitor should notice the close proximity of *Fertile* to *Climax*. The locals claim a woman from the former died in a traffic accident in the latter. A local newspaper could not resist, and ran the headline, "Fertile Woman Dies in Climax."

Use your travels to collect memories of wonderful Minnesota. Visit and recall forever the local dynamism of *Sleepy Eye*. Get out of your rut and experience *Gully*. Steer your boat down aristocratic *Rat Root River* and acquire tales to titillate your sophisticated friends. Savor rememberances of the local joyous spirits at *Downer*. Conclude your tour at *Radium* and remember Minnesota with glowing memories.

Other often overlooked places are *Welcome, Shooks, Zim, Flom,* and *Lude*.

Mississippi

"The Magnolia State"

True Facts and Silly Stats

Population: 2,586,443
Area: 47,234 sq. mi.
Capital: Jackson
State Motto: Y'all Look Suspiciously Like Yankees
State Song: "Go, Mississippi"
State Bird: Mosquito
State Plant: Cotton
State Economy: Cotton
Famous Singer: Elvis Presley
Famous Writer: William Faulkner
Famous Civil War Site: Vicksburg National Military Park
Major Tourist Attraction: Natchez

Outrageous Tour Highlights

Before the Civil War, Mississippi was one of the richest states in the United States. It is now one of the poorest. Its previous wealth can be glimpsed at the beautiful historic river town of Natchez. Natchez is filled with charming old homes. Within Natchez is the historic site of the Grand Village of the Natchez Indians. The Grand Village includes temple mounds which were in use when early French settlers arrived. Vicksburg was the site of a famous siege during the Civil War, and the battle ground can be seen in the Vicksburg National Military Park. The military park also contains an ironclad gunboat sunk during the Civil War and later raised.

MISSISSIPPI

Mississippi is best known for its music and was the birth place of Elvis Presley. The Mississippi Delta is where the Delta Blues originated. Vivid and unusual place-names can still be found in Mississippi. An outrageous tour of Mississippi offers good times from *Yazoo* to *Tupelo*!

Mississippi is a jewel of the Old South. A place where women are treated with deference and true chivalry. However, at *Big Bogue Homo*, the men run scared. But most visitors are impressed by the memorable atmosphere of towns like *Sweatman* and *Piggtow*.

Take the exciting pub crawl trail that starts at *Bourbon* and goes to *Tiplersville*. If you find yourself in *Shivers* and wish to reach *Quitman*, your destinations must include *Hot Coffee* and *Reform*.

The tourist will find unforgettable excitement at *Guntown*, on Highway 45. From there its only a short distance northwest to *Gravestown* for the traveler to reach peace and quiet. Indulge your taste for cosmopolitan experiences in *Bobo*, Mississippi. North of *Bobo* is *Rich* where you can hobnob with *Rich* people.

Conclude your tour of Mississippi at *Endville*, where you can bid a fond farewell to a gem in the diadem of the old South.

Other unusual and often overlooked places to see are *Jug Fork, Puskus Creek, Hushpuckena, Crotts,* and *Scooba*.

Missouri

"The Peculiar State"

True Facts and Silly Stats

Population: 5,137,804
Area: 68,945 sq. mi.
Capital: Jefferson City
State Bird: Bluebird
State Flower: Hawthorn
State Animal: Mule
Famous Crook: Jesse James
Famous Politician: Harry S. Truman
State Motto: Send Them to Jail or Political Office, but Get
    Them Out of This Neighborhood
Famous Writer: Mark Twain
Famous Singer: Chuck Berry
Civil War Tourist Stop: Lexington
Major Tourist Attraction: Ozarks

Outrageous Tour Highlights

Missouri is a lush state of rolling plains and forested hills. It was a primary staging area for westward expansion in the 1800s because it lay at the juncture of two mighty rivers, the Missouri and Mississippi. Large modern cities such as St. Louis and Kansas City have sprung up from small pioneer settlements along these rivers. Yet these cities show little sign of their rowdy and boisterous past. Kansas City was once known as "Old Possum Trot." Both Saint Louis and Kansas City were involved in the early Fur Trade, and were "jumping off" points for immigrant settlement of the West.

MISSOURI

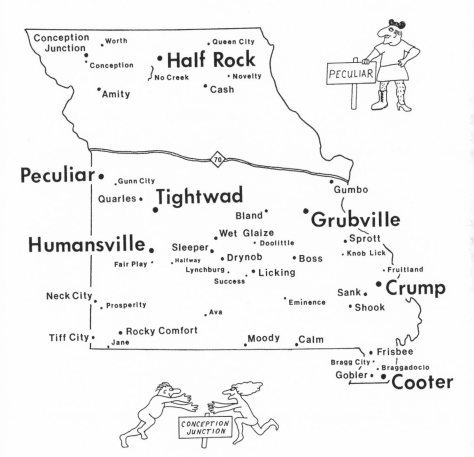

Conception Junction • Worth • Queen City • Half Rock • Conception • No Creek • Novelty • Amity • Cash

PECULIAR

70

Peculiar • Gunn City • Quarles • Tightwad • Bland • Gumbo • Grubville • Wet Glaize • Sprott • Humansville • Sleeper • Doolittle • Knob Lick • Fair Play • Halfway • Drynob • Boss • Fruitland • Lynchburg • Licking • Crump • Success • Sank • Neck City • Eminence • Shook • Prosperity • Ava • Tiff City • Rocky Comfort • Moody • Calm • Jane • Frisbee • Bragg City • Braggadocio • Gobler • Cooter

CONCEPTION JUNCTION

South of these large cities is the scenic hill country of the Ozarks. The spectacular autumn leaves of the Ozarks rival the fall displays of color in New England. Branson, in the Ozarks, is rapidly becoming the country music capital of America and a major tourist attraction.

Missouri is known as "The Show Me State," and Missouri has something to show everyone. Even travelers who think they have seen everything can find *Novelty* in Missouri. In fact, *Novelty* can be found on Highway 156, southeast of Kirksville. The most famous novel place-name in Missouri is *Peculiar*. *Peculiar* is south of Kansas City on Highway 71. A *Peculiar* tour should include a drive past the famed *Peculiar High School* filled with *Peculiar* students. The state of Missouri allows one to go beyond *Peculiar* to *Rocky Comfort* on Highway 76, south of Joplin. There you can enjoy a *Rocky Comfort* bed in a *Rocky Comfort* motel. You can also enjoy a really *Boss* vacation in Missouri. *Boss* is near Dillard Mill State Historic Site.

Many travelers yearn for more than a week or two of vacation diversion. They seek something meaningful and lasting. Such visitors can find what they are looking for in Missouri. For example, who has not yearned for *Fair Play*? You can find *Fair Play* in Missouri south of *Humansville* on Highway 123. *Success* can be found in Missouri at the junction of Highways 17 and 32, east of *Licking*. People who seek *Prosperity* can find it near Joplin, in the southern portion of the state, or one can settle for *Cash* on Highway 3, in the northern portion of the state. Reaching *Cash* or *Prosperity* is usually preceded by a lengthy stay in *Tightwad,* near Macon. After reaching *Success* and *Prosperity* in Missouri, most people go on to the *Eminence* near Ozark National Scenic Riverways. From *Eminence* it is not far to *Braggodocio* and *Bragg City* in the "boot heel" of southeastern Missouri.

The hustle and bustle of Kansas City and St. Louis may make the traveler seek respite. A tourist can find *Calm* along the southern border of the state. Sometimes *Calm* is not enough, and the frazzled travler may seek out *Bland* on Highway 28, southeast of Jefferson City. *Bland* citizens quickly quiet the jangled nerves of the most stressed city dwellers. For those who need more than a *Calm* or *Bland* environment, Missouri offers *Sleeper* on I-44, southeast of *Doolittle*.

The state of Missouri earns its reputation as the "Show Me" state the hard way, at *Conception* located in the northwest. Even more remarkable is the extraordinary location of *Conception Junction* on Highway 136, just north of *Conception*. But if you do not plan on going that far, visit *Halfway* on Highway 32, instead.

Other unusual places to see are *No Creek, Wet Glaize,* and *Dry Knob.*

Montana

"The Holey State"

True Facts and Silly Stats

Population: 803,655
Area: 145,388 sq. mi.
Capital: Helena
Largest City: Billings
State Motto: Sixty Below Zero Keeps Street Crime Down
State Bird: Frozen Chicken
State Flower: Bitterroot
Chief Commodities: Wheat, Coal, and Lumber
State's Most Declined Industry: Buffalo Hunting
Least Successful Visitor: George Armstrong Custer
Major Tourist Attraction: Glacier National Park

Outrageous Tour Highlights

Montana is a vast state with spectacular scenery. The western part of the state holds extraordinary mountain vistas. Glacier National Park is one of the most beautiful in the United States. An hour's drive from Billings is the Custer Battlefield National Monument, site of Custer's last stand.

Montana is one of America's great playgrounds. This state has parks for everyone including those seeking outrageous fun. The tourist looking for the out of the ordinary can stay at wondrous *Hicks Park.* More sophisticated visitors will find attractions beyond their wildest dreams in this paradise of the West, especially if they are connoisseurs of holes. *Big Hole Battlefield National Monument* just goes to show that people will fight over anything. *Hole in the Wall State Recreation Area* is

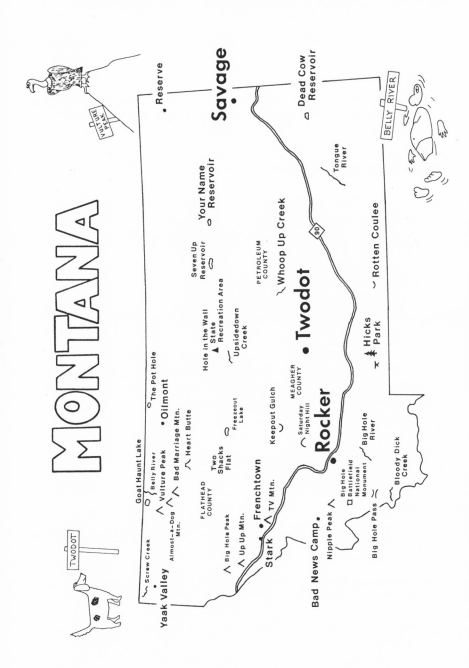

dedicated to the recreational values of holes. The height of hole viewing can be had at *Big Hole Peak,* off Highway 200, near Belknap. Those who would just as soon pass on hole viewing can visit *Big Hole Pass.* If you want to watch things go down a big hole, there is *Big Hole River.* But for people who like holes in their highways, there is *The Pot Hole.*

Anatomy appears to have inspired the citizens of Montana. A state with a place named *Frenchtown* obviously would have a *Tongue River.* Feel the pulse of Montana at *Heart Butte.* Montana's *Belly River* can be found in Glacier National Park. The state has a *Blackfoot* and a *Flathead County. Nipple Peak* proves, what we already knew, that Montana is inhabited by some very lonely ranchers. We don't dare speculate what went on at *Bloody Dick Creek* and *Screw Creek.*

Tourists seeking urbane sophistication will find it at *Two Shacks Flat* in west central Montana. The town of *Twodot* will thrill even the most jaded city slicker bored with one dot towns.

Montana is a place where you can enjoy the only man-made carbonated lake in the world at *Seven Up Reservoir.* As a major livestock producing state, Montana has a storage place for deceased cattle at *Dead Cow Reservoir.* You can visit a reservoir named after yourself at *Your Name Reservoir.*

High altitude couch potatoes will enjoy *TV Mountain* near Missoula. Newlyweds should avoid honeymooning at *Bad Marriage Mountain.* Last but not least, you can see an almost ugly mountain at *Almost-a-Dog Mountain.*

Some other unusual and often overlooked places to see are *Rotten Coulee, Bad News Camp, Whoop Up Creek, Up Up Hill,* and *Upsidedown Creek.*

Nebraska

"A State With Pride"

True Facts and Silly Stats

Population: 1,584,617
Area: 76,639 sq. mi.
Capital: Lincoln
Largest City: Omaha
State Religion: Cornhusker Football
Most Famous Murder: Crazy Horse at Fort Robinson
Most Commonly Heard Phrase: "I'm lost, how do I get to Colorado?"
Famous Persons: Johnny Carson, Fred Astaire, Harold Lloyd, Marlon Brando, Henry Fonda, Montgomery Clift, Gerald Ford, Chief Red Cloud, Buffalo Bill Cody, and Hoot Gibson
Spectacular Fossil Collection: Nebraska State Natural History Museum, University of Nebraska-Lincoln
Best Zoo: Henry Doorly Zoo, Omaha
Leading Phallic Monument: Nebraska State Capitol Building
Major Tourist Attraction: Scotts Bluff National Monument and Chimney Rock Historic Site

Outrageous Tour Highlights

Nebraskans are a proud people. They are proud of everything from their colorful history to their everyday life. If you are driving anywhere in North America and see the people in two cars waving and honking at each other, check the license plates. They are probably Nebraskans greeting each other while away from home. What other state could produce a folklorist like

97

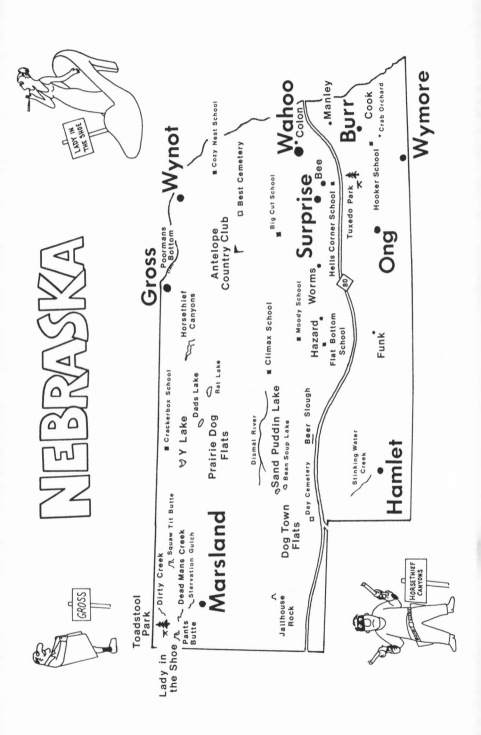

Roger Welsh who celebrates everything in Nebraska from moving houses on flatbed trucks to wearing overalls?

Casual visitors, however, may find such pride inexplicable. Travelers usually describe the drive through Nebraska as "flat and boring." Some describe it as a "living hell," because Nebraska is an exceedingly long state (it is almost 500 miles from Omaha to the Wyoming border). However, just stop and ask a Nebraskan to tell you about the state, and they will regale you with local facts, statistics, lists of famous people, historical events, and curiosities. This verbal bombardment will include everything from the scalping of William Thompson near Lexington in 1867 (an experience he survived) to the beginning of Arbor Day in Nebraska City. These stories are recounted with such sincere enthusiasm that most visitors leave thinking, "Nebraska *is* an interesting place."

Our outrageous tour of Nebraska begins in the east with an exciting visit to *Wahoo*. About five miles north of *Wahoo* is the town of *Colon*. Some tourists quickly pass through *Colon*. Truck drivers proceed carefully, as truck wrecks can lead to a blocked *Colon*. Travelers unable to afford the *Colon* experience stop at *Poormans Bottom*. Those interested in other examples of anatomical topography visit *Squaw Tit Butte*.

Many travelers think of Nebraska as a parched grassland, but numerous rivers, lakes, and streams dot the landscape. The pioneers, impressed by the state's waterways, gave them colorful names. For example, there is *Stinking Water Creek, Dismal River,* and *Dirty Creek* in the western portion of the state.

The refreshing and nourishing possibilities of Nebraska waters did not escape the insight of the pioneers. For example, bring plenty of crackers and enjoy a picnic on the beach at *Bean Soup Lake*, or you could frolic at *Sand Puddin Lake*, then stop for a chaser at *Beer Slough*.

Nebraska has many wonders of nature. *Toadstool Park* draws the hordes of tourists interested in prairie fungi. Actually *Toadstool Park* is a fossil rich area of strange geological formations.

Most travelers crossing Nebraska on Interstate 80 do not

realize they are driving along a geological mystery. Interstate Highway 80, like its forerunner the Oregon trail, follows the Platte River. Visible on the north side of the Interstate are the curious wavelike formations of the "living and moving" Sand Hills. Visible on the south side of the road are the canyon studded loess hills. Scientifically, it is not entirely clear why the sand dunes stop north of the river.

Lovers of wildlife will want to take in *Dog Town Flats, Prairie Dog Flats,* and the city of *Worms.* And Elvis Presley fans will want to see *Jailhouse Rock.*

Nebraska has also maintained the tradition of country schools. Proportionately fewer rural children are bussed to urban areas to attend school than in any other state. In fact, a majority of the nation's remaining country schools are found in Nebraska.

The pioneers named their country schools with the same flair that they named rivers, buttes, and streams. These school names provide outrageous tour possibilities. For example, see *Crackerbox School,* one of the most unusual architectual buildings in the world. See what happens to students who sit too long at *Flat Bottom School.* Truancy is a problem at *Big Cut School.* Other interesting schools are *Hells Corner, Hooker,* and *Climax Schools.* We wonder what prom night must be like at these institutions.

Be sure to visit *Hamlet,* 24 miles west of McCook on Highway 6, which demonstrates the extraordinary imagination used by small town America in naming itself. Foremost among the interesting towns of Nebraska is *Gross,* not far from *Poormans Bottom* in the northeastern portion of the state. The *Gross* citizens will give a *Gross* welcome to any and all visitors. A stay at the *Gross* motel will provide endless stories to regale your friends.

Travelers wishing to get away from it all will find that *Marsland* is an out of this world vacation spot. After a visit to *Marsland,* you can conclude your tour of Nebraska by asking cosmic questions in the sister cities of *Wynot* and *Wymore.*

Other unusual and often overlooked places to see are *Lady in the Shoe, Pants Butte, Dads Lake,* and *Y Lake.*

Nevada

"The State of Chance"

True Facts and Silly Stats

Population: 1,206,152
Area: 109,895 sq. mi.
Capital: Carson City
State Motto: All for Our Country
State Flower: Sagebrush
Main Industry: Gambling
Largest Green Surface in the State: Crap Tables
State Song: "Bing, Bing, Bing"
Unique Law: Legal Prostitution
State Animal: Lounge Lizard
Famous Person: Sarah Winnemucca Hopkins
Major Tourist Attractions: Las Vegas, Lake Tahoe, and Hoover
 Dam

Outrageous Tour Highlights

Spectacular Nevada, an area of great deserts and extraordinary vistas, is one of the major tourist destinations of America. The state is known as a place where a parched land meets an arid land. Because of the dryness, they gave up raising cattle and started raising hell by legalizing both gambling and prostitution. The gambling industry has been a tremendous success. Las Vegas and Reno are the two biggest attractions. Las Vegas, in particular, has an image as an entertainment center of which gambling is a major but not a sole attraction. The spectacular neon light displays of Las Vegas make this city an extraordinary glowing wonder that can best be appreciated at night.

NEVADA

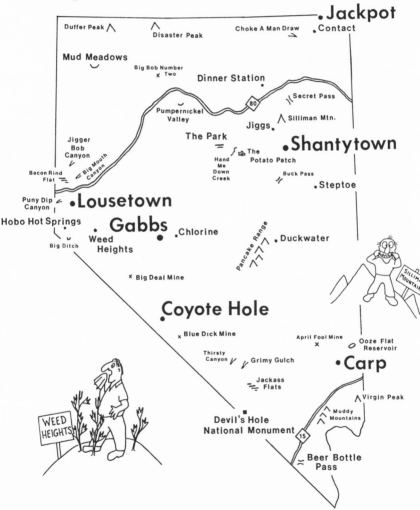

•Jackpot

Duffer Peak ∧   ∧   Choke A Man Draw   •Contact
              Disaster Peak

Mud Meadows

              Big Bob Number
                    x Two   Dinner Station

                                                    .Secret Pass

              Pumpernickel   ⌐80⌐
              Valley   ∧ Silliman Mtn.

                                        Jiggs .

              The Park   •Shantytown
                              ═   ⌐⚙ The
                              Hand   Potato Patch
                              Me
Bacon Rind   ↙Big Mouth   Down   Buck Pass
Flat ═   Canyon   Creek   .Steptoe

Puny Dip ⟋
Canyon   •Lousetown

Hobo Hot Springs   . Gabbs
                                .Chlorine
Big Ditch ⌣   Weed
                    Heights   .Duckwater
                                        Pancake Range
              x Big Deal Mine

                    •Coyote Hole

                    x Blue Dick Mine   April Fool Mine   ○ Ooze Flat
                                                  x   Reservoir
                    Thirsty
                    Canyon ↓ ↓ Grimy Gulch
                                                        •Carp
                              Jackass
                              ═ Flats
                                                        ∧ Virgin Peak
                    Devil's Hole   ∧∧∧ Muddy
                    National Monument ⌐15⌐   Mountains

                                              Beer Bottle
                                              Pass

Because most people come to Nevada to gamble, why not take a chance and visit the other attractions of the state? *Jackpot* in the northeast corner of the state is certainly a desired destination.

In the game of life, miners, whose incomes depend upon discovery, are the biggest gamblers. Miners like gamblers, come to Nevada to strike it rich. Their mines are everywhere. Tourists who don't like to visit inconsequential mines can visit *Big Deal Mine,* south of Hawthorne. You can watch a big strike being made every April first at the *April Fool Mine,* east of Alamo. For a rest stop, you can do what Big Bob does, at *Big Bob Number Two,* north of Interstate 80. We advise both tourists and miners to skip the winter season at *Blue Dick Mine* at the southwestern edge of the state.

Take a chance and enjoy the tourist attraction of *Weed Heights,* off Alternate Highway 95, in western Nevada. No one can say the experience is "nothing to sneeze at."

If you want to take a chance on finding some conversation, you might make a long visit to *Gabbs,* on Highway 361. Those seeking a good giggle should stop at *Silliman Mountain.*

Human ecologists have compared the harshness of Nevada's arid Great Basin climate to the severity of an arctic environment. Nobody has any sort of chance in Nevada without water. Clearly someone overestimated their ability to survive the brutal desert sun at *Thirsty Canyon,* north of Beatty. A parched throat can make a visitor resort to *Duckwater,* east of the *Pancake Range* near the center of the state. The mountains in the *Pancake Range* may resemble pancakes because of dehydration.

There is no need to worry about finding safe water at *Chlorine,* east of *Gabbs,* but watch your eyes in the swimming pools. For a very short swim try *Puny Dip Canyon* near Reno. Those visitors who would like to fish or swim in a used stream can visit *Hand Me Down Creek,* south of Interstate 80, near Carlin. The local mecca for waterskiing is *Ooze Flat Reservoir* east of Elgin. *Ooze* may not be the most attractive waterskiing medium, but it is slick. Other slick skiing experiences can be had at the *Muddy Mountains* northeast of Las Vegas. A place where the tourist can either complain or fish is *Carp,* on a wash north of Lake Mead.

The people who named Nevada places had food as well as water on their minds. Nevada has *The Potato Patch,* near the Cortez Mountains; *Pumpernickel Valley,* south of Winnemucca; *Dinner Station,* north of Interstate 80; *Choke a Man Draw,* in the northeast corner of the state; and finally *Bacon Rind Flat,* north of Reno.

Other unusual places are *Mud Meadows, Coyote Hole, Beer Bottle Pass, Lousetown,* and *Grimy Gulch.*

New Hampshire

"A State of Hidden Passions"

True Facts and Silly Stats

Population: 1,113,915
Area: 8,992 sq. mi.
Capital: Concord
State Bird: Purple Finch
State Flower: Purple Lilac
State Tree: White Birch (they couldn't find a purple one)
State Motto: Kill the Tax Man
State Crop: Rocks
Major Historical Attraction: Strawbery Banke (Portsmouth)
Major Scenic Attractions: White Mountains and the Flume
Most Popular Risque Attraction: Hussey Mountain

Outrageous Tour Highlights

New Hampshire is famous as the first state to declare independence in 1776. The first permanent Euro-American settlement in New Hampshire was Little Harbour (Rye) established in 1623. New Hampshire was once a part of Massachusetts but became a separate colony in 1679. New Hampshire had numerous disputes with its neighbors Massachusetts, Vermont, and Maine. These disputes are historically attributed to disagreements about boundaries. However, the secret, real source of the problem has been the passionate nature of the New Hampshirites. Unlike their Puritan neighbors, the early founders of New Hampshire simmered with barely controlled passions. This is why their neighbors, particularly the

NEW HAMPSHIRE

Happy Corner •　　• Stub Hill

Kidderville •

Goback Mtn. ∧　　∧ Mt. Patience
Stark　　　　• **Chickville**

⌂ Uknown Lake
⌒ The Bulge

⌒ Pond of Safty

Mt. Deception ∧　♫ Crew Cut Trail

Smutty Hollow ~
Bath •　　Lend-A-Hand Trail ∽

⌒ The Bowl

Mt. Cube ∧　Mad River　• North Sandwich
∧ Chick Corner •　• **Center Sandwich**
Sandwich

Blow-me-Down
⌒ Pond

∧ Tumbledown Dick Mtn.

Pokamoonshine Brook
∧ Hussey Mtn.

[93]　Bumfagging Hill

Sodom Hill　　　• **Madbury**
Crotched
Mtn. Ski
Area　Ye Old
Cemetery
□　• Rye Beach
Keene •　　　∧　　**Little Boars Head**
Noone •　Bumbo Hill　• Peppermint Corner
Hittytity Brook

traditional Puritans of Massachusetts, thought it best to segregate such passionate people in the rocky, rugged area to the north. Over the years the people of New Hampshire have cleverly fostered an image of themselves as rugged, stoic people. Their place-names, however, tell a different story.

The outrageous passion tour of New Hampshire begins in the southern portion of the state in *Peppermint Corner*. Not much illicit or raucous activity goes on in *Peppermint Corner* because of the watchful and ever present influence of Massachusetts folk just a short distance away, across the state line. (To experience the full measure of wild New Hampshire exuberance you have to wait until the tour reaches *Happy Corner* at the remote northern end of the state.)

In southern New Hampshire, the tour allows visitors to observe extraordinary examples of public breast beating at *Hittytity Brook*, or join locals in releasing inhibitions at *Madbury*.

During the winter months, the passion tour heads northeast to *Crotched Mountain Ski Area*. This area demonstrates that even the chill of winter cannot cool New Hampshire passions.

In summer, the tour goes directly north to *Hussey Mountain* and *Tumbledown Dick Mountain*. Both seasonal tours stop for *Bath* on Highway 302. This is followed by a wild night at nearby *Smutty Hollow*. Male tour members usually want to visit *Chick Corner* or its sister city in the north, *Chickville*. Women tour members almost always want to see *The Bulge* south of *Stark*.

Strong passions lead to hearty appetites and this is evident in New Hampshire place-names. There is not only a *Sandwich* in New Hampshire, but a *North Sandwich* and a *Center Sandwich* as well. Surprisingly, *Rye Beach* is some distance away in the southeastern corner of the state. After *Sandwiches* you can indulge your sweet tooth by a return to *Peppermint Corner,* bringing our passion tour of New Hampshire full circle.

Note: The state government has attempted to control some of the excesses of its citizens by limiting access to intoxicating beverages. Liquor stores are state owned, and any establishment serving alcoholic beverages has to serve food as well. However, it seems locals may have gotten around this prohibition at *Pokamoonshine Brook.*

Other often overlooked places are *Bumfagging Hill, Blow-Me-Down Pond, Bumbo Hill, Mount Cube, Goback Mountain, Lend-A-Hand Trail,* and *Crew Cut Trail.*

New Jersey

"The Garden State"

True Facts and Silly Stats

Population: 7,748,634
Area: 7,468 sq. mi.
Capital: Trenton
State Bird: Eastern Goldfinch
State Mineral: Concrete
State Tree: Smokestack
State Motto: I Take the Fifth Amendment
Famous University: Princeton
Famous Entertainer: Bruce Springsteen
Hotel-Casino Center: Atlantic City
Major Tourist Attraction: Cape May Historic District

Outrageous Tour Highlights

New Jersey is famous as a hub of industry and transportation. Major highways and railways cross New Jersey linking New York, Philadelphia, Baltimore, and Washington, D.C. New Jersey's location has made it a center of trade and industrial development since the Colonial times. The nation's first model factory town was developed in New Jersey in 1791, in Paterson. Thomas Edison worked diligently at his laboratory in West Orange, New Jersey. His home and lab are now a National Historic Site.

New Jersey has experienced the economic fluctuations and upheavals that accompany industrial development. Visitors can examine the ups and downs of the pharmaceutical industry at *Pill Hill,* near Interstate 287, south of Morristown National

109

NEW JERSEY

LEISURE WORLD

- Rudeville
- Donkeys Corners
- Tranquility
- Hope
- Jenny Jump Mts.
- Lake Just-It
- Nutley
- **Buttzville**
- Mount No More
- **Scrappy Corner**
- Changewater
- Bunnvale
- Pill Hill
- Point No Point
- Peapack Ski Area
- Finesville
- **Pumptown**
- Teeny Weeny Acres
- Leisure World

POINTERS

195

- Buddtown
- Aunt Debs Ditch
- Apple Pie Hill
- **Dicktown**
- Whooping John Creek
- Elephant Swamp
- Chew Road
- Mud Hole Meadow
- **Penny Pot**
- Pointers
- Daretown
- Cat Gut
- Bacon Neck

CHEW ROAD

- Pork Island
  Great Egg Harbor Bay

Poor House Flat
Little Dung Thorofare
Dung Thorofare
Nummytown

Historic Park. An upspring in the local economy is expected at the *Jenny Jump Mountains.* Anticipating an economic boom, New Jersey's remarkable airport, *Teany Weeny Acres,* is planning expansion to accommodate twin engine airplanes as well as the single engine planes and hang gliders it now services. The community of *Penny Pot* is looking to capitalize on inexpensive pay toilets.

Some areas of New Jersey have been in need of redevelopment. Two of these places are *Poor House Flat* and the *Dung Thorofares. Dung Thorofare* poses an especially sticky problem. Of course, *Little Dung Thorofare* poses a smaller problem.

New casinos and hotels have revitalized Atlantic City and made it a place to go for excitement. But the outrageous traveler may want to visit *Whooping John Creek,* on the west side of southern New Jersey, near *Deepwater.* If you don't think *Whooping John Creek* is anything to shout about, not far away is *Dicktown, Daretown,* and *Aunt Debs Ditch.* Certainly, one should not go to *Mount No More,* near *Buttzville,* for amorous adventure. Wholesome entertainment can be found at *Apple Pie Hill* near Chatsworth in the south central portion of the state.

Atlantic City businesses need not worry about competition from developments in northern New Jersey. It is unlikely that tourists will give up summers at Atlantic City beaches to ski on packed peas at the *Peapack Ski Area* west of Newark. The developers of *Peapack Ski Area* aimed for year-round business, but they realized that the color of artificial snow pack does not match a summer landscape, but green peas do. Since one of New Jersey's chief agricultural products is cranberries, developers might look into the possibility of a more colorful Cranberrypack Ski Area. Cranberries also take the grueling impact of ski jumping events better than peas.

Despite New Jersey's small size, as American states go, it is a feisty state. According to historical accounts, an early period of lawlessness in New Jersey ended in the 1750s when the people became involved in the the French and Indian War. The state's feisty tradition is still evident at *Scrappy Corner* not far from

Allamuchy Mountain State Park. If *Scrappy Corner* does not provide the visitors with enough excitement, try exchanging insults with the tourist information bureau at *Rudeville.*

Finally no matter what one thinks about New Jersey, the state is not without *Hope. Hope* can be found in New Jersey just off Interstate 80, near the Pennsylvania border.

Other often overlooked places to see are *Mud Hole Meadows, Donkeys Corners, Lake Just-It,* and *Elephant Swamp.*

New Mexico

"The Land of Enchantment"

True Facts and Silly Stats

Population: 1,521,779
Area: 121,336 sq. mi.
Capital: Santa Fe
Largest City: Albuquerque
State Motto: At Least It's Dry Heat
Climate: Has some advantages relative to an oven
State Bird: Roadrunner
State Flower: Yucca
Famous Outlaw: Billy the Kid
Spectacular Pueblo Indian Village: Acoma
Average Indian Family: Father, Mother, Two Children and an
    Anthropologist
Major Tourist Attraction: Carlsbad Caverns

Outrageous Tour Highlights

New Mexico is a land of contrasts. The scenery blends blue-rimmed mesas with shimmering deserts and forested mountains. The state combines the rich heritage of Indian, Spanish, and Anglo-American cultures. Even the state's climate is one of variety. Temperatures rise or fall five degrees with every 1,000 ft. of elevation. There are corresponding differences in rainfall at different elevations. These climatic contrasts support six different life zones, rich in plant and animal diversity.

New Mexico's cultural heritage combined with summer temperatures reaching 110 degrees make New Mexico one of the hottest vacation destinations around. In the northeast

113

NEW MEXICO

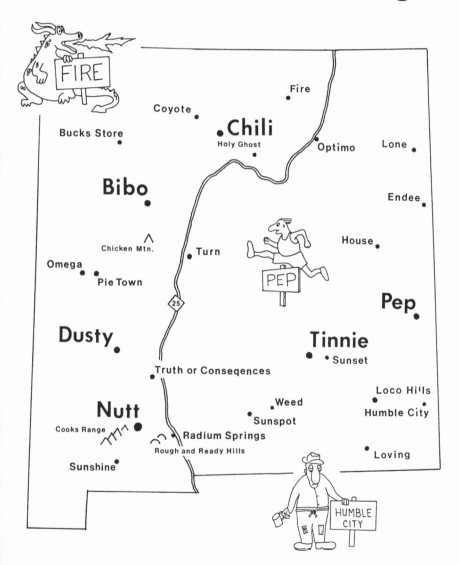

FIRE

Fire

Coyote

Bucks Store

Chili

Holy Ghost

Optimo

Lone

Bibo

Endee

Chicken Mtn.

Turn

House

Omega

Pie Town

PEP

Pep

Dusty

Tinnie

Sunset

Truth or Conseqences

Loco Hills

Nutt

Weed

Humble City

Cooks Range

Sunspot

Radium Springs

Rough and Ready Hills

Loving

Sunshine

HUMBLE CITY

25

portion of the state, you can experience both the warmth of the climate and the warmth of the people, in *Fire*. *Fire* is located on Highway 434, east of Taos. Males in town are known as *Fire Men*. Of course, it is illegal to shout the name of the town in a crowded room. In winter, you can try skiing at the nearby *Angel Fire Ski Area*. With winter temperatures in New Mexico averaging almost 40 degrees, *Fire* in the ski area is provided to ensure that the skiers hurry down the slopes with or without the benefit of snow.

After warming up in *Fire*, you can drive south for lunch and gas at *Chili*, near Los Alamos. You can stop for dessert at *Pie Town* on Highway 60. Relax and sit by the window of the local cafe and watch the crusty residents filling *Pie Town*. Continuing south you will come upon *Cooks Range*, a must for outdoor enthusiasts.

New Mexico has been a leader in scientific research and energy development. Los Alamos and Sandia Laboratories are world famous in the fields of nuclear, solar, and geothermal energy research. Although you may be interested in touring one of these famous labs, we suggest you visit one of the outrageous scientific laboratories in New Mexico. Try cheering the spirits of the lonely scientist working at the *Lone* Laboratory in *Lone*, New Mexico. Tour the *Bibo National Laboratory* not far from the Laguna Indian Reservation and find out what's new in *Bibo* research. Travel to the well-known Roswell Industrial Air Center if you want, but the *Tinnie* aircraft proving grounds near *Tinnie*, New Mexico, are guaranteed to be more exciting. Engage in your own nuclear research by drinking at *Radium Springs*. The experience will fill you with an inner glow, in quite a different way than a visit to *Loving*, New Mexico.

A typical New Mexico town is *Dusty*, on a dirt road between *Omega* and *Truth or Consequences*. Shop in the *Dusty* stores. Enjoy the *Dusty* cuisine of the local restaurants. Remember, in *Dusty*, a brushoff is not an insult. Drop in at the library and check out the *Dusty* books. Another New Mexico town travelers should consider visiting is *Weed* on Highway 24, east of Alamogordo.

New Mexico gives you a chance to practice your assertiveness training with impunity in *Humble City.* Stop at the town's restaurants for their special dish, *Humble* pie. Visit the extraordinary sister sites of *Nutt* and *Loco Hills.*

There are a few tips for the New Mexico traveler. Forget about listening to the radio when you drive past *Sunspot.* Take care to avoid sunburn at *Sunshine.* And remember, you can get out of the sun at *Sunset.*

With so much to see and do in New Mexico, it is easy for the traveler to become exhausted. The tired and weary traveler should find *Pep,* located south of Portales on Highway 206.

In order to get the most out of your New Mexico vacation stop at *Optimo. Optimo* is south of Wagon Mound on Interstate Highway 25. After experiencing *Optimo,* most travelers are convinced that New Mexico is "a little bit of heaven." This can be verified by visiting *Holy Ghost. Holy Ghost* can be found north of Glorieta on Interstate 25. Conclude your New Mexico tour at *Endee.*

Other unusual and often overlooked places are *Rough and Ready Hills* and *Bucks Store.*

New York

"Empire State"

True Facts and Silly Stats

Population: Huddled masses yearning to breathe free (18,044,505)
Area: 47,379 sq. mi.
Capital: Albany
Largest City: New York City
State Motto: We Are All There Is, Except for a Few Frontier Outposts Like L.A.
State Song: "I Love New York"
State Bird: Bluebird
State Tree: Street Lamp
State's Tallest Skyscrapers: World Trade Towers
State's Favorite Skyscraper and King Kong Perch: Empire State Building
Best Natural Scenery: Hudson River Valley
Best Skyline: Manhattan Island
Best Waterfall: Niagara Falls
State Mugger Preserve: Central Park
Best Tourist Advice: Avoid sightseeing during the rush hour.
Major Tourist Attraction: New York City

Outrageous Tour Highlights

New York City is known as the preeminent American city. It is America's center of fashion, theater, publishing, communications, manufacturing, commerce, and finance. The image of New York City is so overwhelming that many people in the West and Midwest think of New York State as an island packed with

117

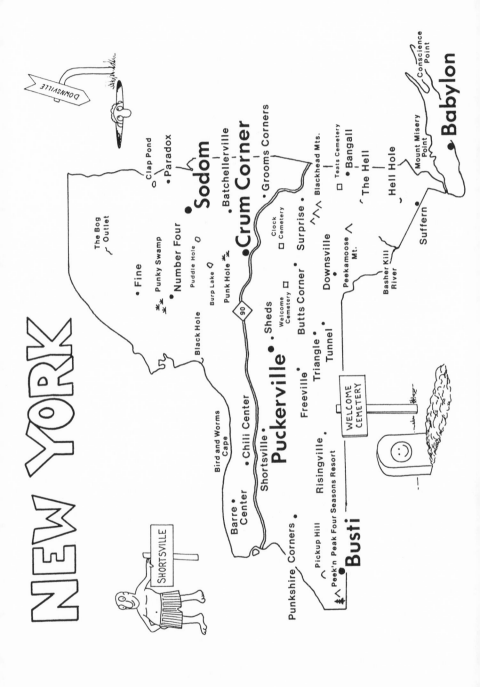

skyscrapers. Few people in the "hinterland" realize New York State is as wide as Nevada (both 320 miles in maximum breadth). New York State has a big, brash, outrageous "hinterland" beyond the limits of Manhattan. Here are some of the state's outrageous places.

You can find what you never expected in New York at *Surprise.* The state's *Surprise* can be found north of Hudson on Route 81. Attend the town's celebrations and you have attended *Surprise* parties. The local schools are famous for giving *Surprise* exams.

If you are traveling north on Interstate Highway 87 and miss the *Surprise* exit (Route 81/385), you may find yourself in *Paradox,* New York. The town's politicians claim to spend their time solving *Paradox* problems. Dealing with *Paradox* problems is considered good experience for politicians hoping to run for state office.

People from the Midwest think that anything goes in New York. This is, of course, true. There are no stuffed shirts in *Babylon* east of New York City on Long Island. New Yorkers are very forthright about their lack of inhibitions at *Sodom* near scenic Highway 28, in the northern portion of the state. If Midwesterners think *Sodom* is a raucous place, they should visit *Bangall* north of New York City. At *Busti,* south of Jamestown, men can check out *Busti* women. Tours for singles stop at *Pickup Hill,* north of *Busti,* for dates before heading to *Puckerville* near the center of the state. Voyeurs of large animals enjoy *Peekamoose Mountain* west of Kingston. Those who want to take a peek all year around prefer *Peek'n Peak Four Seasons Resort* in the extreme southwest corner of the state. The presence of these outrageous places may explain why the state has a *Conscience Point* located on the tip of Long Island.

For the very best vacation, visit *Fine,* on Highway 3, in the northern portion of New York. In addition to *Fine* restaurants, the primary attraction is the *Fine* judicial system which tries *Fine* criminals. The community of *Fine* is presently hosting sanitation researchers from New York City. The reason for the research visit is that this town is able to maintain a *Fine* landfill, and has no problems keeping sanitation workers happy and strike free with *Fine* garbage.

New York State has its share of natural wonders. The most spectacular is the mysterious *Black Hole* near Pulaski. It is rumored that state and local funds have disappeared in this *Black Hole,* and it is responsible for the state's financial difficulties.

Prices can be high in New York City, but New York State offers a variety of economical alternatives. Why pay astronomical prices for a hotel room or apartment in Manhatten, when low-cost accommodations are available in *Sheds* on Highway 13, southeast of Syracuse. Although New York City is a fashion center, there is no need to budget for clothes in *Barre Center* south of Albion in the western portion of the state.

New Yorkers don't have to travel to the Midwest or Far West to find a *Hell Hole.* New York has one near *Popolopen Lake* west of Peekskill. If New York State's *Hell Hole* is not sufficiently stimulating, residents of the Big Apple can experience *The Hell* on a weekend excursion near Hyde Park north of Poughkeepsie.

Unlike out-of-state visitors to New York, the dead always receive a warm greeting at *Welcome Cemetery* near Morris.

Other unusual places you might want to visit are *Punky Swamp, Puddle Hole, Burp Lake, Bird and Worm Cape, Clock Cemetery,* and *Teats Cemetery.*

North Carolina

"The Tar Heel State"

True Facts and Silly Stats

Population: 6,657,630
Area: 48,843 sq. mi.
Capital: Raleigh
State Motto: Not Smoking Is Harmful to Our Economy
State Flower: Dogwood
State Tree: Pine
First Airplane Flight: The Wright brothers at Kitty Hawk
First Lost Luggage: The Wright brothers at Kitty Hawk
Famous Entertainer: Andy Griffith
Famous Preacher: Billy Graham
Unusual Church Services: Snake Handling
Scenic Drive: Blue Ridge Parkway
Spectacular Beach: Cape Hatteras National Seashore
Major Tourist Attraction: Great Smoky Mountains National Park

Outrageous Tour Highlights

The beautiful coast of North Carolina attracts visitors with its spectacular beaches and barrier islands. Roanoke Island was the site of the first English settlement in the Western Hemisphere. Lovely mountains in the western part of the state offer the visitor excellent scenery and camping opportunities.

North Carolina also offers visitors stimulating and outrageous vacation possibilities. Have a blast at *Salvo*. Get a bang out of *Boomer* and *Shooting Creek*. *Seven Devils Resort* offers everyone a hell of a vacation. Or visit the *New Found Mountains* and marvel at how they could have overlooked those big things.

121

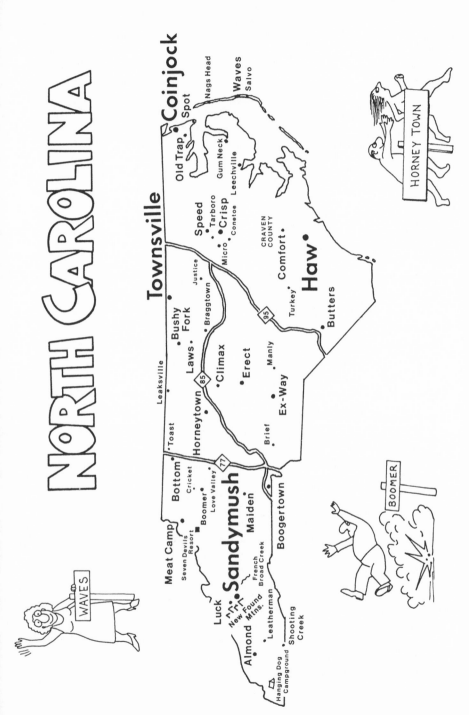

Whether you are traveling alone or with a group, North Carolina has a vacation destination right for you. The divorced head for *Ex-Way*. The elderly are caught up by beguiling *Old Trap*, where quaint shops preserve the romantic past of tourism with items such as brightly colored "home sweet home" pillows and Indian moccasins.

Savor the character of the state's people. Their originality and creativity can be gauged by the names they have used to describe their hamlets, such as *Townsville*. Anatomical peculiarities of inhabitants are immortalized at places such as *Nags Head*, *Gum Neck*, and *Conetoe*.

If you search for *Justice*, you'll find it in North Carolina. Canine criminals receive especially quick justice at *Hanging Dog Campground*.

Experience North Carolina's high cuisine. Stop at *Toast* for breakfast. After a fire, the town is known as burnt *Toast*. Most natives prefer *Crisp*, on Highway 258. Continue your tour of North Carolina with cholesterol raising experiences at *Butters*. The state's low fat alternative destination is *Turkey*, on Highway 24. For something more gritty than grits, try *Sandymush*. Few visitors are aware that the foul-mouthed eccentric in *Almond* is known as the salty nut. It is recommended that vegetarians pitch their tents somewhere other than *Meat Camp*.

Recapture the essence of romance in North Carolina. Become enraptured by the beauty of *Maiden* and *French Broad Creek*. The atmosphere can become steamy in *Horneytown*, so be sure to request a motel with a cold shower. If you travel from *Love Valley* to *Erect*, it is not far to *Climax*.

Here are a few tips for the North Carolina traveler. If you are looking for good fortune, search for *Luck*. When you are out of *Luck*, you may reach *Bottom*, on Interstate 77. But don't despair, you can find *Comfort* in North Carolina, found east of *Pink Hill* on local route 41.

Other unusual places are *Haw*, *Cricket*, *Micro*, *Brief*, and *Boogertown*.

North Dakota

"The Peace Garden State"

True Facts and Silly Stats

Population: Less than several people
Area: 69,299 sq. mi.
Capital: Bismark
Largest City: Fargo
State Bird: Western Meadowlark
State Flower: Wild Prairie Rose
State Tree: Telephone Pole
Climate: Compares favorably to dry ice
State Motto: Thawing Is for Sissies
Major Industry: Ice Cube Manufacturing
Famous Person: Louis L'Amour
Major Tourist Attraction: Theodore Roosevelt National Park

Outrageous Tour Highlights

Many people assume that North Dakota had a quiet evolution into statehood. Peacefully tucked along the Canadian border, North Dakota was far from the hubbub of the Oregon and Santa Fe trails. Texas cowboys never drove herds of cattle to wild railhead cowtowns in North Dakota. In fact, some people assume nothing exciting ever happened in the state until Lawrence Welk was born in 1903. Actually, North Dakota has a colorful history. Explorers, fur traders, and the U.S. military followed the Missouri River north and west to North Dakota. Famous Indian tribes inhabited the area: the Mandan, Hidatsa, and Dakota (Sioux). Fort Union, established in 1829 by the

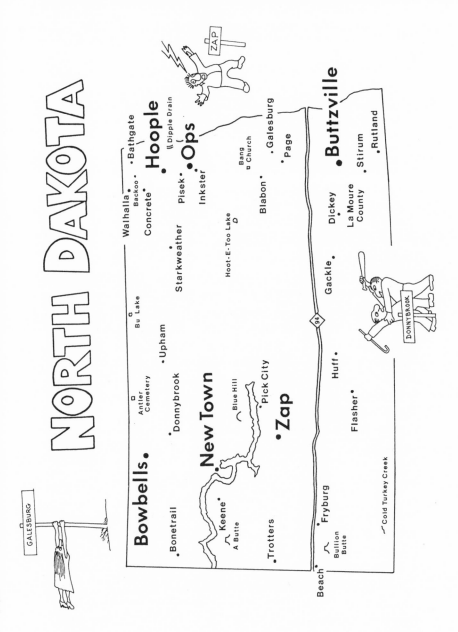

NORTH DAKOTA

GALESBURG

ZAP

DONNYBROOK

Bowbells.

• Bonetrail

Keene•
⌒ A Butte

• Trotters

• Donnybrook

New Town
•

⌒ Blue Hill

• Pick City

•Zap

• Antler
Cemetery

• Upham

□ Bu Lake

Starkweather

Hoot-E-Too Lake
⌒

Walhalla•
Backoo•
Concrete•

Pisek•

Inkster•

•Bathgate

•Hoople
((Dipple Drain

•Ops

Blabon•

Bang
□ Church

• Galesburg

• Page

•Buttzville

• Stirum

• Rutland

Dickey
•

La Moure
County

Gackle
•

94

Huff •

Flasher•

• Fryburg

⌒ Bullion
Butte

• Beach

⌒ Cold Turkey Creek

American Fur Company, was one of the most important and colorful outposts on the American Frontier.

Despite a colorful history, early developers thought that North Dakota might not attract settlers. An attempt was made to make the state more enticing by changing place-names. The capital of North Dakota was originally named Edwinton. But the name was later changed to Bismark in the hope of attracting foreign investment and immigrants. A perusal of North Dakota place-names indicates the name "Edwinton" was the least of the state's "problem" place-names. For example, consider *Ops, Hoople, Inkster,* and *Zap.* But North Dakota may have no need to worry. It is unlikely that foreign investors comprehend American place-names. *Bonetrail, Bowbells,* and *Gackle* may sound as inviting to Japanese investors as the names Grand Forks, Mapleton, and Gladstone. Nevertheless, considering an outsider's fear of extremes in North Dakota weather, it is probably best that the communities of *Starkweather* and *Galesburg* change their names immediately. Promising substitute names might be Balmyweather and Belle Air. We suggest the name *Cold Turkey Creek* be changed to *"Comfortable" Turkey Creek.*

As far as investment is concerned, buyers may want to consider a few "outrageous" properties. The most highly recommended locale for development in North Dakota is *Pick City.* Investors and corporate directors looking for modern facilities may want to set up shop in *New Town. Keene,* of course, has the *Keene* industrial park. Investors can obtain a revealing glimpse of the real North Dakota by visiting *Flasher.* If you are scouting out North Dakota, do not tear through *Page*—it's the only one they have. Finally, developers should be aware that *Buttzville* is one town that is all it's cracked up to be.

Most corporate heads are concerned about the cultural and recreational opportunities available in an area before building a new plant or moving the company's headquarters. There is no need to worry in North Dakota. The state is famous for hunting and fishing opportunities. Exciting boxing matches are held at

Donnybrook. Lovers of music can take in the concerts at *Hoot-e-Too Lake.* Executives and employees alike can relax after a day's work at *Bu Lake.* And, last but not least, people always feel up in *Upham.*

As far as place-names and development go, there is some food for thought. If the town named *Walhalla* did not attract Teutonic immigration and investment of major proportions, nothing will.

Interestingly, the town of *Dickey,* North Dakota, is not located in *Dickey County. Dickey* apparently preferred to be in *La Moure County.*

Other often overlooked places are *Bang Church, Antler Cemetery, Dipple Drain, Bullion Butte,* and *Blue Hill.*

OHIO

"The Beaucoup de Ville State"

True Facts and Silly Stats

Population: 10,887,325
Area: 41,004 sq. mi.
Capital: Columbus
Largest City: Columbus
State Motto: So Far From Heaven, So Close to West Virginia
State Tree: Buckeye
State Flower: Scarlet Carnation
State Book: *Goodbye Columbus*
Most Depressed Industry: Amish Car Dealerships
State Conservation Miracle: Restoration of Carp to Lake Erie
Famous Generals: Ulysses S. Grant and William Sherman
Major Tourist Attraction: Lake Erie Islands

Outrageous Tour Highlights

The name "Ohio" is an Iroquoian term which implies something fine or great. The term is taken to refer specifically to "great river." Over the years Ohio has been a "great state," a leader in both industry and agriculture, a home of inventors, manufacturers, and seven presidents. With such a remarkable history, it is little wonder that America's *"Pulse"* is found in Ohio.

The community of *Pulse*, Ohio, is located south of Highway 50, near Danville. The people of Ohio keep an eye on their *Pulse*, because, as historic leaders in invention and industry, they are a fast moving people. In fact, Ohioans are always on

OHIO

FOOTVILLE

FLEATOWN

FLUSHING

• Zone
• Luckey
Hicksville•
Celeryville•
• Rushmore   Widowville•   • Funk
    • Meeker   • Richville
Gutman•   Jelloway
Rushsylvania•   • Charm
    • Bangs
    Mutual•   Flushing•   • Rush Run
Tradersville•   Outville   Salesville•
Goes•   • Fleatown   • Dilles
Frytown•   Freeland•   Temperanceville•   Bottom
Gratis•   Rushville•   • Crooksville   Round
    Robtown•   Bottom
    PICKAWAY   • New Straitsville
    COUNTY   Stringtown
Mount Healthy   Guysville•
    • Pulse   Dyesville•   Coolville
Tightwee   Letart Falls
    Rushtown•   • Kitchen
    Greasy Ridge

71

Footville•
Remindersville•
• Delightful

Shgo•

the go. This is evidenced by the town of *Goes* on Highway 68, east of Dayton.

A proclivity for fast living is evidenced by a typical tour of Ohio places. Fast tours begin in the southern portion of the state at Portsmouth on the Ohio River. Tours head north to *Rushtown*, located on scenic route 104. The tour buses travel to *Rushtown* via four-lane Highway 23, instead of scenic Highway 24, because the less scenic route enables the tourist to reach *Rushtown* more quickly. After a brief stop at *Rushtown*, tours hurry north to *Rushville* east of Lancaster. No one is allowed to get off the tour buses because *Rushsylvania* is next on the itinerary. The pace of the tour quickens to include *Rush Run* on Highway 7, and *Rushmore*, off Highway 189. *Rush Run* and *Rushmore* are on opposite sides of the state, but a fast tour pace makes up for less than ideal routing. *Tightwee* and *Flushing* are potential rest stops when you rush around Ohio.

Ohio has been one of America's most successful melting pots, combining the descendants of settlers from Connecticut, Virginia, and Kentucky with immigrants from a host of European countries. Prominent during the abolition movement prior to the Civil War, Ohio was the first state to have an interracial, coeducational college (Oberlin, 1833). This ethnic and cultural diversity may explain why Ohio has a "ville" for everyone. The suffix "ville" can mean a place of a specific nature. Ohio has a *Coolville* for those who are "in" and an *Outville* for those who are not. There is *Dyesville*, for those who are looking for a community with color. Ohio's *Temperanceville* bars are renowned for serving water on the rocks. Men live in *Guysville*, while Ohio widows live in *Widowville*. Hopefully these two towns will get together. The people of *Reminderville*, southeast of Cleveland, will remind you to hold on to your wallet when you visit *Crooksville*, in the southern portion of the state. Graduates of the *Robtown* high school do well in *Richville*, south of Canton. Tourists who want to shop for bargains are advised to go to *Salesville* east of Cambridge. But if you want to swap, go to *Tradersville* west of Columbus.

Ohio offers the outrageous traveler a host of other colorful communities. Travelers can unravel in *Stringtown*. Visit the real estate offices in *Freeland*, and discover that the town's name is false advertising. Visit the town of *Delightful*, where you can examine their *Delightful* sewer system, check out their *Delightful* garbage trucks, and look over the accommodations at their *Delightful* jail. At *Charm*, Ohio, children attend a *Charm* school. You can tour *Zone*, Ohio, during the day, but sunset is the best time to visit, then you can see the twilight *Zone*.

The dining places in Ohio are legendary. Ohio cuisine is best appreciated at *Kitchen* on Highway 233, north of *Greasy Ridge*. Dieters should head for *Celeryville*, south of Willard on Highway 224, and *Jelloway* on Highway 3.

Conclude your visit to Ohio by observing the remarkable anatomical characteristic of the residents of *Round Bottom* on route 536, southeast of Cambridge. Then blush for Mr. Dilles at *Dilles Bottom* on Highway 7.

Other often overlooked places are *Mount Healthy*, *Bango*, *Fleatown*, and *Funk*.

Oklahoma

"The Sooner State"

True Facts and Silly Stats

Population: 3,157,604
Area: 68,656 sq. mi.
Capital: Oklahoma City
State Bird: Scissortailed Flycatcher
State Flower: Mistletoe
State Cloud: Dust Cloud
State Tree: Oil Derrick
State Motto: Labor Omnia Vincit (Labor Conquers All Things)
Famous Humorist: Will Rogers
Famous Singer: Woody Guthrie
Good Cowboy Museum: National Cowboy Hall of Fame
Good Indian Museum: Cherokee Heritage Center
Famous Empty Building: Museum of Oklahoma Erotica

Outrageous Tour Highlights

Oklahoma is famed as the land of American Indians and oil. The boom and bust cycle of the oil business has likewise affected the state economy. Tourism is now second only to oil in the state's economy. The eastern part of the state is hilly and forested, providing great opportunities for outdoor recreation. Many Indians were moved to the Oklahoma area from east of the Mississippi by the Federal government. The result is a mosaic of various Indian cultures in the state.

Oklahoma is famous for football and is known nationally as the site of the Dust Bowl. In the eastern portion of the state, the Ozark Mountain foothills attract sportsmen. The success of bird

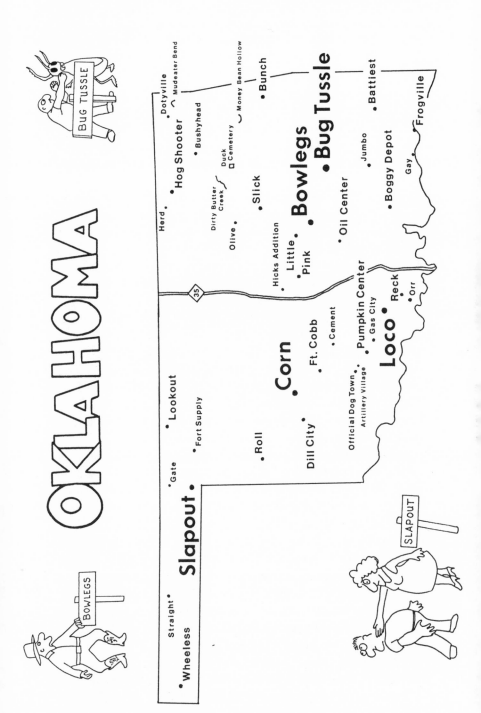

hunters can be judged by *Duck Cemetery.* If a visitor's taste in firearm excitement runs to bigger things, we recommend *Artillery Village,* at Lawton. A stay at *Artillery Village* should satiate the most jaded gun enthusiasts. For those who like violence without mechanical innovations, there is *Slapout,* Oklahoma. Travelers are advised to go to *Lookout,* before wandering into *Slapout.* If hand to hand combat with insects is your thing, visit *Bug Tussle,* near McAlester.

Follow Oklahoma's famous psychology trail for a madcap good time. Stay overnight at *Dotyville* in their famous padded motel rooms. Visit *Loco* and discuss flying saucers and the paranormal with the *Loco* populace. For an even crazier time, stop at *Battiest.* The *Battiest* citizens will amuse you with their high jinks. With towns named *Straight* and *Gay,* no one can say that Oklahoma does not offer a choice. You can go to either *Straight* or *Gay* bars.

If you are looking for a place to buy a house, there is *Hicks Addition* near Oklahoma City. To the south, on Route 65, you can go slumming in the seedy section of *Pumpkin Center.* Many people have apparently searched for *Dog Town* in Oklahoma, but don't put up with unofficial substitutes, demand to stay at *Official Dog Town,* near Lawton.

Oklahoma is well known as a mecca for the aristocratic. Jet setters will want to stop at *Boggy Depot.* Too long a stay at *Boggy Depot* can make one a candidate for residence in nearby *Frogville.* When you croak in that town, they either put you in the pond or in the cemetery.

Oklahoma cuisine has become a legend. Enjoy the state's entire culinary repertoire at the towns of *Corn, Olive, Dill City,* and *Oil Center.* Then stop at *Cement* for a little light dessert. For inexpensive food and exercise, stay at *Mudeater Bend.* Discover the lower price spread at *Dirty Butter Creek.*

The physical beauty of Oklahomans is legendary. You can always spot the beauty pageant contestant from *Bowlegs,* Oklahoma, especially during the swimsuit event. If you look pretty in *Pink,* why not enter the local beauty contest?

Be careful with your car at *Reck.* Visit the historic section of town, which is known as old *Reck.* Guess what car trouble you can expect in *Wheeless.* It is difficult to get to *Roll* from *Wheeless.* If you smash your car at *Gate,* Oklahoma, you'll be known as a *Gate* crasher.

Other unusual, often overlooked places are *Money Bean Hollow, Hog Shooter, Slick,* and *Fort Cobb.*

Oregon

"The Remote State"

True Facts and Silly Stats

Population: 2,853,733
Area: 96,187 sq. mi.
Capital: Salem
Largest City: Portland
State Motto: Chop It Down and Sell It to the Japanese
State Bird: Western Meadowlark
State Flower: Oregon Grape
State Tree: Stump
Historic State Conflict: Sheepmen and Cattlemen
State Fear: Invasion by Californicators
Great Scenery: Columbia River and Mount Hood
Major Tourist Attraction: Oregon Coast

Outrageous Tour Highlights

Oregon has forests in the west and dry prairie in the east. Portland, its major city, is an attractive metropolitan area with a number of interesting museums. The spectacular Columbia River Gorge is just outside Portland, and is prettiest in the fall. The rugged Oregon coast is exceptionally beautiful and large areas are protected as state parks.

Oregon is a state of lumbermen and ranchers who have played an interesting role in the naming of Oregon places. Visit *Three Fingered Jack Mountain*, where Jack, a lone prospector, learned the hard way not to make rude hand gestures to the local loggers. Savor the cosmopolitan charm of *Remote*, where the city fathers brag that *Remote* is the chance for wealth,

136

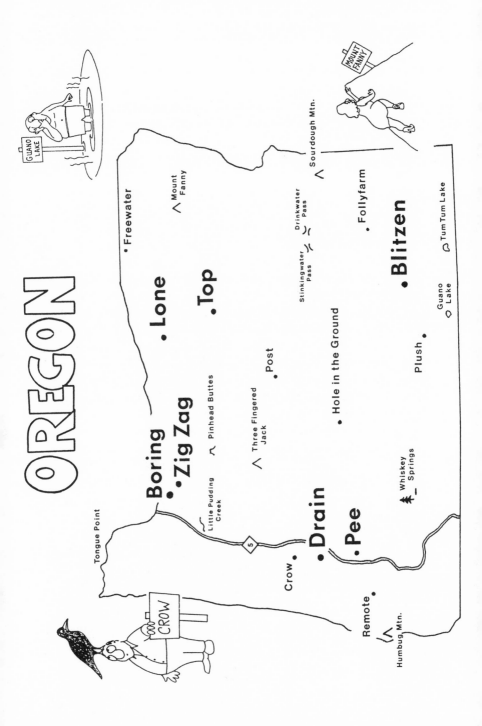

power, and fame. Elbow your way through the surging throngs of *Lone,* where the town bachelor is the *Lone* lonely man.

The pristine water quality of Oregon is legendary. Oregon has *Crater Lake,* which is noted for its beautiful blue color and as being the deepest lake in America. But tourists who want to avoid crowds, visit Oregon's outrageous lakes. Take a swim in *Guano Lake.* You don't need to make reservations at *Guano Lake,* just be like everyone else and drop in. Look before you dive, though. The lake is located in the arid eastern half of Oregon and is usually dry. There is nothing that chafes the body like a belly buster onto dry Guano.

TRAVEL TIP: It is best to fill your canteens and water jugs at *Drinkwater Pass* because you won't like what you find at *Stinkingwater Pass.*

Oregon can provide the discriminating tourist with dining experiences of a lifetime. It is alright to eat at *Crow,* which is certainly better than eating crow. Guess what is on the menu of the diners around *Sourdough Mountain?* The cultured palate of the gourmet will enjoy the high calorie water of *Little Pudding Creek.* If you drive after visiting *Whiskey Springs,* you'll soon go to *Zig Zag.*

The following are a few final tips for an outrageous tour of Oregon. Watch the moon rise over *Mount Fanny.* See unsuccessful farming practices demonstrated at *Follyfarm.* We suggest you avoid spending the Christmas season at *Humbug Mountain.* And, if you have traveled too long without a rest stop, you will find relief at *Pee,* which is not far from main Route 5. But if you miss it, it is only a short distance north to *Drain.*

Other unusual, often overlooked places are *Hole in the Ground, Pinhead Buttes,* and *Tongue Point.*

Pennsylvania

"America's Hometown State"

True Facts and Silly Stats

Population: 11,924,710
Area: 44,892 sq. mi.
Capital: Harrisburg
Largest City: Philadelphia
Most Renewed City: Pittsburgh
Famous Person: Benjamin Franklin
State Motto: Go Fly a Kite
Most Famous Reference: W. C. Field's epitaph, "On the whole, I'd rather be in Philadelphia"
State Bird: Ruffed Grouse
State Flower: Mountain Laurel
The State's Least Feared Criminal Organization: Amish Mafia
Name Origin: Pennsylvania is derived from the last name of William Penn and the first name of Sylvester Stallone, two of the state's most prominent citizens.
Major Tourist Attraction: Independence Hall and National Historic Park

Outrageous Tour Highlights

Pennsylvania is fondly thought of as America's hometown. The actor Jimmy Stewart, a native of the state, epitomizes the good nature and quiet charm associated with Pennsylvania. The state has many pleasant places to call home. There is *Good* on Highway 997, north of Waynesboro. The town is filled with *Good* citizens, *Good* children, and *Good* pets. Then there is *Goodville*, south of Reading. The town of *Hometown* can be

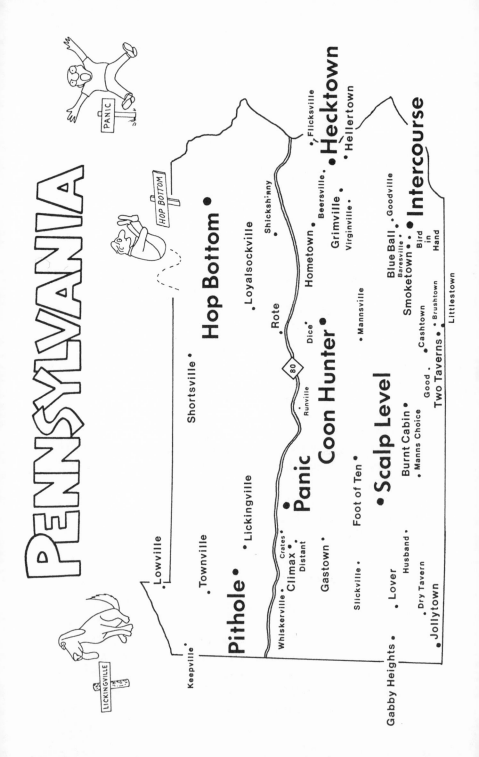

found at the junction of Highways 309 and 54, east of Mahanoy City. At *Hometown,* you can have a hometown of *Hometown.* You can also root for the hometown *Hometown* baseball team. Another community whose name says it all is *Townville,* on Highway 408. *Gabby Heights* is also a congenial place to visit.

Despite the wealth of hometown goodness in Pennsylvania, one should not assume that the citzens of the state are meek or mild. A trip to *Hellertown* near the New York border will make that clear. Pennsylvania folk can be hell raisers, but they rarely use bad language in *Hecktown.* Other places the rambunctious traveler might want to see while in Pennsylvania are *Dice, Two Taverns,* and *Beersville.*

Sports enthusiasts will enjoy Pennsylvania. Track fans flock to *Runville,* which sponsors the world's only perpetual marathon race. Pennsylvania also offers something unique for basketball fans. If you are tired of seeing tall basketball players casually drop balls in baskets, the Pennsylvania dwarf basketball playoffs bewteen *Shortsville* and *Littlestown* are for you. There are other unique sports events in Pennsylvania such as the unusual track and field events at *Hop Bottom* on Highway 11, north of Scranton.

Some people like to spend their vacation helping others. If public service is your goal, Pennsylvania is for you. At *Foot of Ten,* you can help the citizens count their toes. Or, you can help the residents of *Burnt Cabin* build a new one. Volunteers are always needed to spread sand on the streets of *Slickville,* east of Pittsburgh.

Pennsylvania is one state where you can experience a paranormal event. Although scientists have studied the mysterious phenomenon, they cannot explain it, nor have they been able to harness it for use in other American cities. This phenomenon is the physical impossibility of losing a sock while doing laundry in *Loyalsockville.*

Most people familiar with American places know that *Intercourse* can be found in Pennsylvania. However, very few tourists, bewildered by the maze of Pennsylvania roads, have the nerve to approach someone on the street and ask how to get to *Intercourse*. We will give you a hint: it is east of *Lover*. Unfortunately, *Intercourse* is located on a secondary road. If freezing winter weather prevents you from getting to *Intercourse*, you can reach *Blue Ball*, via Primary Highway 322. Presumably, people of *Virginville* could never reach *Intercourse*. Most travelers interested in *Intercourse* hope to conclude their tour in *Climax*, Pennsylvania. However, given Pennsylvanian modesty, there is no easy way to reach *Climax*. It is at the other end of the state.

Other unusual, often overlooked places to visit are *Bird in Hand, Coon Hunter,* and *Scalp Level.*

Rhode Island

"The Mystery State"

True Facts and Silly Stats

Population: 1,005,984
Area: 1,054 sq. mi.
Capital: Providence
Claim to Fame: The Tiniest State
State Motto: Excuse Me, But Your Foot Is Covering My Estate.
State Tree: Dwarf Willow
Tourist Attraction: Newport Mansions
State Sport: Yacht Racing
Only Business Opportunity: Small Business
Immigration Problem: When one fat person enters the state, two
     thin people have to leave.
Famous Person: George M. Cohan

Outrageous Tour Highlights

Rhode Island is America's smallest state. It's maximum
length and breadth is 48 × 37 miles. Those distances will not
get a traveler from one highway rest area to the next in most
other states. Rhode Island is so small that a map approaches the
actual size of the place. Crammed in to this tiny area are over a
million residents. There are over 75 cities and towns with
structures that support a million people. Residential homes are
not limited to high-rise apartments or tiny one-room cabins.
Rhode Island is known for palatial mansions and estates of the
wealthy. There are 399,000 acres of forested land, and Rhode
Island has enough additional land for the horticultural production of potatoes, apples, and turf. Most amazing of all, there are

RHODE ISLAND

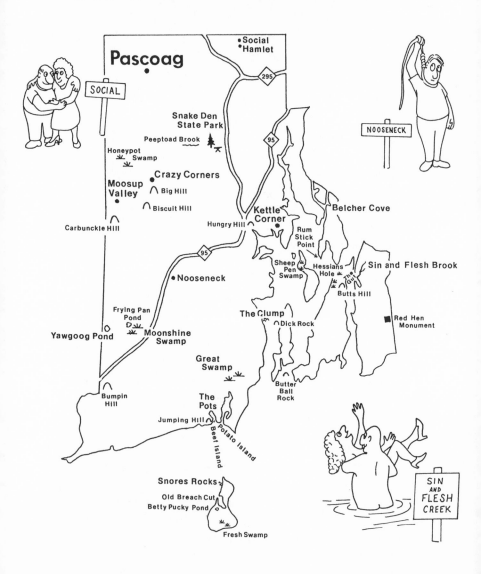

Social
Hamlet

Pascoag

SOCIAL

NOOSENECK

Snake Den
State Park

Peeptoad Brook

Honeypot
Swamp

Crazy Corners

Moosup
Valley   Big Hill

Biscuit Hill

Kettle
Corner   Belcher Cove

Carbunckle Hill   Hungry Hill   Rum
Stick
Point

95

Sheep
Pen
Swamp   Hessians
Hole   Sin and Flesh Brook

Nooseneck

Butts Hill

Frying Pan
Pond   Red Hen
Monument

Yawgoog Pond   Moonshine
Swamp

The Clump   Dick Rock

Great
Swamp

Bumpin
Hill   Butter
Ball
Rock

The
Pots

Jumping Hill

Snores Rocks

Old Breach Cut
Betty Pucky Pond

SIN
AND
FLESH
CREEK

Fresh Swamp

an incredible number of swamps in the state. How can so much be in a place so small? This is the mystery of Rhode Island. Visitors sometimes assume that because of Rhode Island's small size, yachting is the only adventurous activity in the state. However, visitors need not study the art of sailing. There are numerous possibilities for wilderness adventures in Rhode Island. The most outrageous of these are swamp tours.

The most impressive Rhode Island swamp is *Great Swamp* between Highways 2 and 110. Louisiana may have alligators in its swamps, but Rhode Island has sheep, especially at *Sheep Pen Swamp* south of Providence. There is nothing like the smell of wet wool to convince you that you are in the great outdoors. A professor of biology personally guides tours of the *Sheep Pen Swamp* and provides informative lectures on sheep pen behavior.

Louisiana has colorful Cajuns and great Cajun cooking. But there are colorful residents of Rhode Island swamps as well. These cagey swamp denizens are *Hessians*. Most are found in *Hessians Hole* north of Newport. They speak a unique language because they have been isolated in Rhode Island swamps since the Revolutionary War. Their cuisine is also uniquely different. They make ingenious use of vinegar and spices in the preparation of traditional cabbage dishes. *Hessian* guides are available for most Rhode Island swamp tours. Midnight *Hessian* drinking tours are available at *Moonshine Swamp*. There has been criticism that tours have disturbed the wildlife ecology in the most visited areas. A Rhode Island swamp that is still pristine is *Fresh Swamp* on Block Island.

In Louisiana, one can tour the *Honey Island Swamp*, where a swamp monster has been sighted. Rhode Island also has its share of swamp monsters. These are giant half human, half apelike beings that have terrified visitors to the swamps. The most famous is the *Honeypot Swamp* monster. *Honeypot Swamp* is located north of *Moosup Valley*. *Crazy Corners* is the staging site for *Honeypot Swamp Tours*. Ask your hotel concierge for details.

If swamps and monsters are not what your are looking for, Rhode Island has other interesting places. There is *Snake Den State Park,* east of Providence, and *Jumping Hill,* south of Highway 1. Both are guaranteed to stimulate the visitor.

Rhode Island has other nonswamp water attractions. You can skinny dip to your heart's content at *Sin* and *Flesh Brook.* But, it is recommended that you wear a swimming suit, if you wish to avoid voyeuristic amphibians at *Peeptoad Brook.*

Rhode Island's small size brings people together. Nowhere is this more evident that at *Social,* in the northeast corner of the state, where one can have many interesting *Social* experiences. A visit to a bar there can lead to *Social* drinking. While you are there, take the opportunity to visit with the *Social* hermit, the *Social* miser, and the *Social* misanthrope. Don't get sick there, because you may be accused of having a *Social* disease on your return home.

When traveling Delaware Highway 1, rest room facilities are available in abundance at *The Pots.* Beware of the toilet paper at *Old Breach Cut.* When concluding a tour of Rhode Island, be sure to visit *The Clump* and find out what it is a clump of.

Other unusual places to see are *Snores Rocks, Betty Pucky Pond, Bumpin Hill,* and *Rum Stick Point.*

South Carolina

"A State You Can Count On"

True Facts and Silly Stats

Population: 3,505,707
Area: 30,207 sq. mi.
Capital: Columbia
State Motto: North Carolinians Seem Like Yankees to Us
State Tree: Anything tall, covered with Kudzu
State Flower: Yellow Jessamine
Historic City: Charleston
Olive Drab Theme Park: Paris Island U.S. Marine Base
Famous Person: Strom Thurmond
Major Tourist Attraction: Historic Charleston and Charleston
    Gardens
Spring Break Destination: Myrtle Beach

Outrageous Tour Highlights

South Carolina is famous for its coast. Tourists are drawn to the elegantly beautiful coastal city of Charleston. This city has one of the United States' major concentrations of historic buildings. Visitors should tour the famed historical district. The Civil War began with an attack on Fort Sumter near Charleston. Myrtle Beach, to the north of Charleston, is a major coastal development catering to vacationing university students on mid-term breaks and tourists from the northeast. A number of interesting plantations can be toured between Myrtle Beach and Charleston. South Carolina also offers an array of colorful place-names for an outrageous tour of America's eighth state.

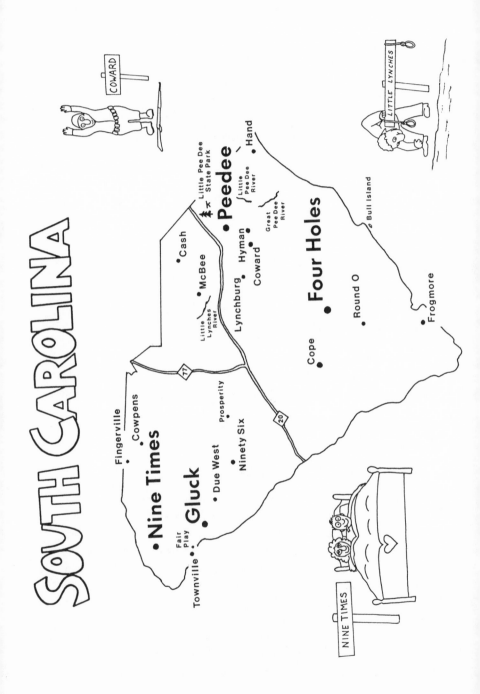

South Carolinians are fond of their "ciphering" skills and have demonstrated these abilities in naming places. For example, north of Charleston is the town of *Four Holes,* which claims to have the shortest golf course in the world. The establishment of *Ninety-Six,* on Highway 34, proves beyond a doubt that they can count that high. Not far from the town of *Six Mile,* in the western part of the state, is the neighboring community of *Nine Times. Nine Times* is noted as the home of the state's sexual athletes. However, the record keeping interval covers a span of a decade.

South Carolinians are also fond of their writing skills, but they have not reached agreement on how this process should be standardized. This is demonstrated by the town of *Round O,* which shows that this alphabetic convention is not universal in the state.

It is easy to follow Horace Greeley's advice to "go west, young man" in South Carolina. You can reach *Due West* by going southeast from *Gluck.* If you want to live a long life, visit *Coward.* They have only *Coward* criminals who will give you no trouble. Visit *Bull Island,* where the state's national politicians are quarantined during Washington recesses. Enjoy the cherry season at *Hyman.*

Don't fail to visit *Peedee.* If that is too overpowering for you, there is *Little Pee Dee State Park,* and *Little Pee Dee River.* If you desire more, there is the *Great Pee Dee River.*

Other often overlooked places are *Fair Play* and *Cowpens.*

South Dakota

"Coyote State"

True Facts and Silly Stats

Population: 699,999
Area: 75,956 sq. mi.
Capital: Pierre
State Motto: We Fought the Indians for a Place With Winters Like This?
State Flower: Pasque Flower
State Bird: Ringnecked Pheasant
State Mineral: Gold
State's Largest Busts: Mount Rushmore
State's Most Disastrous Card Player: Wild Bill Hickock
Best Defoliated Scenery: Badlands National Park
Major Tourist Attraction: Black Hills

Outrageous Tour Highlights

South Dakota has a variety of attractions that draw large numbers of tourists. The delightful pine forests of the Black Hills offer a refreshing contrast to the parched western plains. Mount Rushmore, in the Black Hills, presents giant patriotic sculpture that can be viewed from a number of different beautiful vantage points along a road with hairpin curves.

The Black Hills have many of the attractions of the Rocky Mountains, only existing at a more human scale. Families camping with youngsters particularly enjoy the gentler landscape and terrain of the Black Hills.

Wall Drug, in the town of *Wall,* near *Badlands National Park,* is an enormous store, which has over 2,000 visitors a day.

150

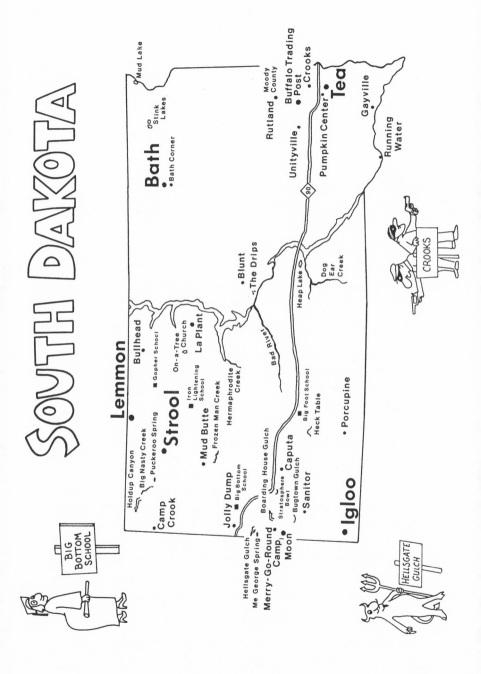

You can buy almost anything at *Wall Drug,* even things you never imagined existed. Another outrageous place to shop is *Buffalo Trading Post,* where you can see what you can trade for a buffalo.

Shoppers in South Dakota should be aware of a few tips. Never buy a car at *Lemmon.* If you buy a used car at *Caputa,* be sure to get an extended repair warranty. Hang on to your billfold when you visit *Crooks,* and be sure to put a dead bolt lock on your tent if you stay at *Camp Crook.*

Believed to be a cold, arid steppe by uninformed outsiders, South Dakota is actually a watery paradise for the outrageous traveler. What visitor could resist a dip in *Bad River* or a splash in *Big Nasty Creek* or *Dog Ear Creek?* If you visit *Mud Butte,* wear waterproof boots.

The need to deal with strong seasonal shifts in climate in South Dakota has created a distinctive personality type. The citizens of *Sanatorium* are crazy about life. *Sanatorium* was apparently too long a word, because the name of the town has been changed to *Sanator.*

The ferocious winters of the state can be truly appreciated at *Igloo.* Be sure to reserve a room in *Igloo* if you visit during the summer, because accommodations during that season get scarce.

The best known towns in South Dakota are *Spearfish,* which hosts the Black Hills Passion Play, and *Deadwood,* which is a National Historic Landmark. Mitchell, in the eastern part of the state, has the curious *Corn Palace.* Outrageous places in South Dakota are *Moon,* where the visitor can be the butt of crude jokes, and *Bullhead City,* where you will never win an argument. At *Stratosphere Bowl,* have an "out of this world" sports experience.

The residents of *Jolly Dump* are happy with their situation. This town appears to have been named by someone from *Blunt.* You'll never guess what sort of people you're likely to meet at *The Drips.*

South Dakota has a number of interesting schools. There is *Iron Lightening School* between *Faith* and *Thunder Butte.*

Youngsters with particular anatomical characteristics are educated at *Big Foot School* and *Big Bottom School.* At *Gopher School,* you can watch children gnaw their way through the school lunch program. Anyone can study diction at the Tarzan School of Public Speaking at *Me George Spring.*

Conclude your tour of South Dakota with a visit to one of the most unusual religious sites in the world, *On-A-Tree Church,* near *Parade,* on Highway 212.

Other unusual places are *Pumpkin Center, Hermaphrodite Creek, Puckaroo Spring, Holdup Canyon, Frozen Man Creek,* and *Heck Table.*

Tennessee

"The Volunteer State"

True Facts and Silly Stats

Population: 4,896,641
Area: 41,154 sq. mi.
Capital: Nashville
Largest City: Memphis
State Motto: Shoot It, Skin It, Eat It
Best State Topographic Feature: Dolly Parton
The Only Place Where Elvis Hasn't Been Seen Lately: Graceland
Famous Frontiersman: Davy Crockett
Country Music Mecca: Nashville
Glowing Attraction: Oak Ridge National Laboratory
Major Tourist Attraction: Great Smoky Mountains National Park

Outrageous Tour Highlights

Tennessee is a very popular state with tourists. The Great Smoky Mountains National Park is easily the most visited of all national parks. Wildflowers are a beautiful attraction in the spring, in the Great Smoky Mountains, and the autumn leaves are a spectacular fall attraction. Nashville, the capital, is a major country music center. The largest city, Memphis, is the site of Elvis Presley's home. Tennessee is also the home of rugged individualists. Many of the men who fought for the the freedom of Texas, including some who died at the Alamo, were actually from Tennessee. The most famous of these were Sam Houston and Davy Crockett. Davy Crockett was well liked for his sense of

TENNESSEE

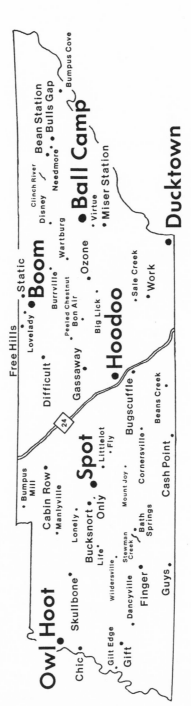

SPOT

DANCYVILLE

BUGSCUFFLE

Free Hills

Static
Lovelady • **Boom**

Clinch River • Bean Station
Disney • Needmore • Bulls Gap
Wartburg Bumpus Cove

Burrville
Peeled Chestnut
Bon Air
Difficult •
Gassaway
Big Lick
Hoodoo
Ozone

Ball Camp
• Virtue
• Miser Station

• Sale Creek
• Work

Ducktown

Bumpus Mill •
Cabin Row •
• Manlyville
Lonely •
Bucksnort •
Life' Only •
Spot
Littlelot
• Fly
Mount Joy •
Cornersville •
Bath Springs
Stewman Creek
Wildersville
• Dancyville
Finger

24

Bugscuffle •
Beans Creek •

Cash Point •

Owl Hoot
Chic •
Skullbone •
Gilt Edge •
Gift •
Guys •

humor. Original Tennessean humor is still evident in the state's colorful place-names.

This state is justly famous for its rural scenery. It is also filled with magnificent urban vistas such as the town of *Spot* south of Interstate 40, between Jackson and Nashville. Not far from *Spot* is *Only*, where you can have a singular vacation. Any child born at *Only* is an *Only* child. If you don't like *Only*, travel north to *Lonely*. Find out where all the *Lonely* people come from. Once there, you can be part of the *Lonely* crowd.

The sophisticate will seek out *Bugscuffle* and stay at night in the local motel, where one can engage in the town sport of scuffling with bugs. *Bugscuffle* is between Manchester and Shelbyville. If you like *Bugscuffle,* you are sure to like *Fly,* near Theta. The yearly dance there is known as the *Fly* ball. If your toes get to tapping, *Dancyville* awaits.

For a challenging vacation, go to *Difficult,* Tennessee, where you can experience the distinctive *Difficult* vacation. Get a new angle on life at *Cornersville.* Or take an economy vacation at *Miser Station.*

Tennessee is rapidly becoming a hub of commerce and industry. Five Interstate Highways link Tennessee with other states. Opportunity awaits for those wishing to get ahead, at *Skullbone,* on Route 105. Tennessee is one place were you can always find *Work. Work* can be found north of Chattanooga. And, don't let anyone tell you there isn't *Life* in Tennessee. *Life* in the state is near Lexington and Jackson.

Tennessee has experienced a six percent growth in population in the last decade. Young adults and new residents who are interested in purchasing a home will find that there are are many real estate opportunities in Tennessee. Visit *Littlelot,* a place with room to grow. Explore the wonderful residential tracts at *Cabin Row.* Real estate in *Disney* is known as *Disney* land. A town in Tennessee that is sure to grow is *Wartburg,* on Highway 27. For a bargain on a waterway visit *Sale Creek.* Travel to *Free Hills* and pick up your free topographic feature.

Tennessee has something for everyone. Shop for the latest fashions at *Chic* or *Gift. Peeled Chestnut,* north of Highway 70, is a convenient and nice place to eat. Get your bumpus ground at *Bumpus Mill.* Dock your bumpus at *Bumpus Cove.* Help scientists find out where and why *Ozone* is disappearing, south of Interstate 40. And, if you have become jaded by the world's other places, learn to give a hoot in *Owl Hoot.*

Some other unusual places to visit are *Finger, Stewman Creek, Boom, Static,* and *Hoodoo.*

Texas

"A Whole Other Country"

True Facts and Silly Stats

Population: 17,059,805 plus Mexico
Area: 262,015 sq. mi.
Capital: Austin
Largest City: Houston
State Motto: You Can Find a Lot of B.S. on and In Our Cowboy
   Boots
State Flower: Bluebonnet
State Tree: Pecan
State Bird: Corporate Jet
Origin of State Name: Indian word meaning "those white guys
   can sure tell whoppers"
Best Beach: Padre Island National Seashore
Best Last Stand: The Alamo
Best Urban Stretch of River: River Walk in San Antonio
Major Tourist Attraction: Big Bend National Park

Outrageous Tour Highlights

"It's like a whole other country" is the tourism slogan of
Texas. Not only is Texas big enough to be a whole other country,
it is big enough to be a whole *lot* of other countries. The state of
Texas is bigger than the combined areas of Great Britain,
Ireland, the Netherlands, Belgium, Switzerland, Denmark, Aus-
tria, and Hungary. Six different national flags have waved over
Texas during its history. These were the flags of Spain, France,
Mexico, the Republic of Texas, the Confederacy, and the U.S. If
the size and history of Texas are not enough to convince a visitor

TEXAS

Dial

Twitty

Happy
New Loco
Loco
Happy Gasoline
Needmore Union
Barwise
Circle Back
Heckville
Close City
Petty
Justiceburg
Gunsight
Noodle

Telephone
Selfs
Wolfe City
Frog Hop
Loving
Drop
Hicks Cash

Tarzan
Tool
Gun Barrel City
Cow Flats
Retreat
Looneyville
Bangs
Pancake
Coit
Cut
Flat
BELL
Ding Dong
COUNTY
Grit
Old Dime Box
Snook
Dime Box
Cut and Shoot

Feely
Mission
Concepcion
Cost
Needville
Cheapside
Bigfoot
Nursery
Coy City
Peggy
Zunkerville

Concepcion

TARZAN

BIGFOOT

CUT
AND
SHOOT

that Texas can be a whole other country, an outrageous tour of Texas place-names will.

The traveler should experience the "frontier country" of Texas. One of the most notorious gunmen of the Old West, John Wesley Hardin, was born in Bonham, Texas, in 1853. Hardin claimed to have killed 44 men. Not far from Hardin's home town is *Gun Barrel City,* off Highway 175, southeast of Dallas. Another colorful place is *Gunsight* between Abilene and Fort Worth. A Texas place-name that says it all is *Cut and Shoot,* located on Highway 105, north of Houston. *Cut and Shoot*'s sister city is *Bangs,* west of Brownwood in the central portion of the state. Gunfights stopped at *Bangs* only when public pressure for noise abatement grew intense.

Another Texas to experience is the "romantic country." Visitors in search of *Loving* can find it on Highway 16 south of Wichita Falls. Ladies are advised to stay in *Coy City* in the southern part of the state, because cowboys usually come from *Wolfe City* in the north. One can visit the Texas town of *Coit,* and experience its coital pleasures. Love tours of Texas usually end in *Concepcion* southwest of *Nursery.*

Another Texas to experience is the "country of high finance." Texas is a leader in agriculture, industry, and technology. State revenues of 33 billion dollars are exceeded only by the revenues of California and New York. But unlike California and New York, Texas's revenue is achieved without a state income tax. A visitor can learn the secrets of Texas's financial success by touring the state's outrageous economic centers. Texans save most of their money by contracting with businesses from *Cheapside,* west of Yoakum. Texans save state and local funds by avoiding waste. For example, the town of *Old Dime Box* has not been abandoned despite the development of a newer *Dime Box.* Plans are being developed to merge the Texas communities of *Cut* and *Cost.* Be sure to take in *Cash,* northeast of Dallas, because missing *Cash* is a problem for any tourist.

Another Texas to experience is the "wild and crazy" country. The wild and crazy intellectuals of *Twitty,* Texas, will amaze you, particularly the *Twitty* librarian and *Twitty* teachers. While in *Loco,* study the *Loco* community development plans. If you crave more madcap adventures, head for *Looneyville.* The town of *Barwise,* north of Lubbuck, has the only *Barwise* minister in the state.

Texas is one country that is big enough to have both *Bigfoot* and *Tarzan.* Real swinging Texans find *Tarzan* on Highway 176, west of *Big Springs.* If you prefer an ape to an ape-man, you can find *Bigfoot,* off Interstate 35 south of San Antonio.

If you find yourself going around in circles on your Texas tour, you have probably reached *Circle Back* northwest of Lubbock. You can go to *Dial* or *Telephone* for directions. A gang of crooks in *Telephone,* Texas, is known as a *Telephone* ring. But for a different kind of ring in Texas visit *Ding Dong,* located in *Bell* County north of Austin.

Texans are also famous supporters of the military. The citizens of *Retreat* are one hundred percent behind the military and getting more so.

Conclude your tour of Texas by leaving *Happy* on Interstate 27.

Other often overlooked places to see are *Mission Conception, Cow Flats,* and *Frog Hop.*

Utah

"The Beehive State"

True Facts and Silly Stats

Population: 1,727,784
Area: 82,076 sq. mi.
Capital: Salt Lake City
State Motto: We Can Raise 12 Lizards to the Acre
State Bird: Seagull
State Tree: Blue Spruce
Most Difficult Business Venture: Mormon Bars
State Proverb: No Alcohol, No Smoking, No Caffeine and You'll
    Live Long, or At Least It Will Seem That Way.
Natural Engineering Wonders: Natural Bridges National
    Monument
Largest Body of Water: Great Salt Lake
State Name Origin: Indian word meaning "no fun at all"
Famous People: The Osmonds
Major Tourist Attraction: Zion National Park

Outrageous Tour Highlights

Utah is a destination for those who relish the beauties of nature. Utah has five national parks and six national monuments. Although Utah has only one national recreation area, Glen Canyon National Recreation Area, it is the second largest in the U.S. (1,236,880 acres). Zion National Park is located near Interstate Highway 15. This makes Zion an easy destination for tourists. Other areas such as Canyonlands National Park are reached via secondary roads and are less visited. If you enjoy going off the beaten path, an outrageous tour of Utah is for you.

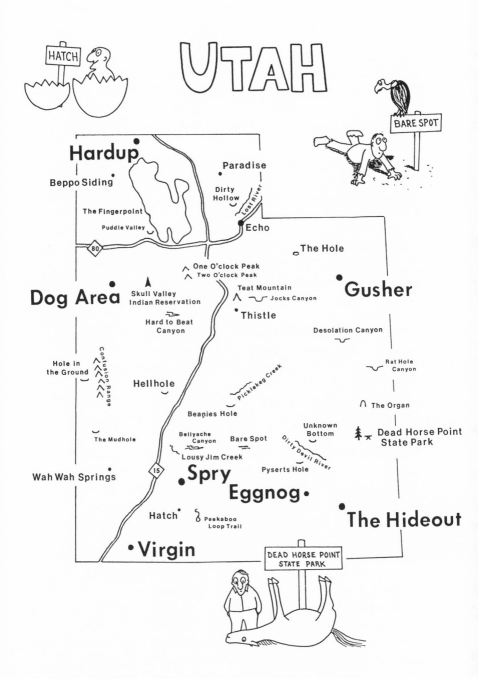

The most pristine place in Utah is *Unknown Bottom,* somewhere between *Dirty Devil River* and *Dead Horse Point State Park.* Few, if any tourists have ever visited *Unknown Bottom,* primarily because it is unknown. Other little visited areas in Utah are *Pyserts Hole, Lousy Jim Creek,* and *Desolation Canyon.* Tour schedules need to be arranged carefully in order to be on time to glimpse *One O'clock* and *Two O'clock Peaks* west of Interstate 15, near Ophir. We would also like to point out *The Fingerpoint* in the northeast portion of the state. We can assure the modest traveler that it is not pointing at *Teat Mountain.*

Utah's scenery involves distant horizons and a full spectral range of colors. Such grandeur can tire the eyes. If your eyes become tired, you can give them a rest by gazing at Utah's *Bare Spot. Bare Spot* is not far from Highway 24, near Torrey and Bicknell.

Utah is a state known for aridity. One of the most famous desert areas in the U.S. is Utah's 4,000 square mile Great Salt Lake Desert. Some areas of the state receive as little as five inches of rain a year. The visitor may encounter quaint variations in speech patterns among local residents. This is due to parched throats caused by the aridity. Visit *Wah Wah Springs* and find out. There you can join the locals in slurping down a tall glass of wah wah. You will find that *Lost River* is not lost at all, people simply drank it up. The town of *Gusher* was named after a drinking fountain in the city park where people came from miles around to see running water. *Puddle Valley,* near the Great Salt Lake Desert, is the local mecca for water sports.

Many people travel to Utah to enjoy the food. Utah cuisine owes its unique and hearty flavor to the simple tastes and values of the pioneers. Never a wordy people, the menus are clear and straightforward. During the holiday season, most travelers stop for a drink at *Eggnog.* However, most travelers avoid the diners at nearby *Bellyache Canyon.*

Utah has many interesting communities. The town of *Virgin,* near Zion National Park, is famed for its *Virgin* maternity ward. Not far away is *Spry,* where you can visit the *Spry* old folks home. Relax and come out of your shell at *Hatch*, Utah. Did you know that the town of *Paradise* has a *Paradise* dump? Learn why Indians are not pleased with their living conditions at *Skull Valley Indian Reservation*.

Utah is the only state in the U.S. that has twenty-one places named Hell Hole. This is why visitors say, "You are never far from a hell hole when you are in Utah." If you don't like hell, but you do like holes, Utah offers *The Hole*. There is *Hole in the Ground* for earthy types. Those who get mired down will like *The Mudhole. Dog Area* is for those finding their vacation going to the dogs.

Some other unusual, often overlooked places are *Peekaboo Loop Trail, Dirty Hollow, Beppo Siding, Picklekeg Creek,* and *Hard to Beat Canyon.*

Vermont

"The Rugged, Quiet State"

True Facts and Silly Stats

Population: 564,964
Area: 9,273 sq. mi.
Capital: Montpelier
Largest City: Burlington
State Motto: It Takes Grit to Farm Rocks
State Flower: Red Clover
State Bird: Hermit Thrush
State Sticky Stuff: Maple Syrup
Principal Crop: Yankee Republicans
Major Exported Resource: Crushed Rock
State's Golden Orator: Calvin Coolidge
Major Tourist Attraction: Green Mountain National Forest
Famous Empty Building: Vermont Center for Carnal Knowledge

Outrageous Tour Highlights

Vermont is the archetypal New England state. Its forested mountains are major attractions in the fall, with the brilliant autumn foliage drawing huge numbers of tourists. During the winter, ski resorts bring more tourists. Anytime of the year, visitors can enjoy the picturesque villages that dot the landscape. Vermont is famed for the exploits of Ethan Allen and the Green Mountain Boys during the Revolutionary War.

The citizens of Vermont are stereotyped as rugged individualists who don't speak much. This does not mean that they are mentally incapable of speech. Some are even said to be able to

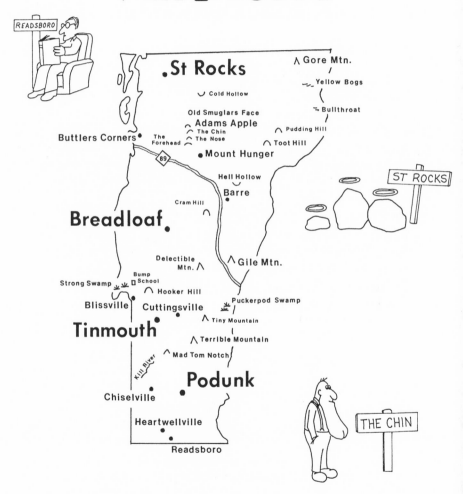

read, for example, the people of *Readsboro*. However, their taciturn nature is legendary. The town of *Tinmouth* memorializes the petrification of the speech organs that often besets the state's citizens. The honesty of their utterances can be judged at *Bullthroat*. The alleged stodginess of Vermonters would not seem to apply to the residents of *Barre*. The *Barre* minister and the *Barre* church choir save plenty of money on robes and vestments.

The splendor of Vermont's rugged vastness must be seen to be appreciated. Tourists will stare with mouths agape as they view the wonder of *Hell Hollow*. Of course, for a really good vacation there is always a weekend on *Terrible Mountain*.

Those searching for a pleasant vacation will head straight for *Blissville*. A pilgrimage to *Heartwellville* will make you feel warm all over. *Breadloaf* is for those who have spent too long on *Mount Hunger*. Those wishing to assuage other hungers will want to visit *Hooker Hill*.

Those who named Vermont places were clearly inspired by anatomy. The cerebral will want to visit *The Forehead*. From *The Forehead* you can travel nearby to *The Nose*. *The Nose* is usually picked as one of the state's most remarkable attractions. Of course, not far from *The Nose* is *The Chin*, and not far from there is the *Adams Apple*.

Other unusual places are *Puckerpod Swamp, Mad Tom Notch, St. Rocks, Yellow Bogs, Pudding Hill*, and *Cram Hill*.

Virginia

"The Society State"

True Facts and Silly Stats

Population: 6,216,568
Area: 39,700 sq. mi.
Capital: Richmond
Capital of the Confederacy: Richmond
Largest City: Virginia Beach
State Motto: Someone in a Three Cornered Hat Slept Here
State Flower: Dogwood
State Tree: Dogwood
State Song: "Carry Me Back to Old Virginia"
State Holy Relic: George Washington's wooden false teeth
Major Tourist Attraction: Mount Vernon
Historic Restored Town: Williamsburg
Major Industries: Rolling Cigarettes and Tourists
Claim to Fame: Has the bedrooms for both George Washington
     and Washington, D.C.

Outrageous Tour Highlights

Virginia represents one of the greatest concentrations of historic sites in the United States. Virginia was one of the first English speaking colonies in America. Most of the early presidents of the United States lived in Virginia. Richmond was the capital of the Confederacy during the Civil War, and much of the fighting during that war took place in Virginia. With such a rich cultural and historic heritage, most travelers overlook the possibility of finding outrageous places in Virginia.

169

VIRGINIA

ASSAWOMAN

BIRDNEST

CUCKOO

Assawoman
Ticktown
Frogstool
Birdnest

Butts Corner
· Dumfries

Butts
Odd
Driver ·
Cheesecake Cemetery
Ordinary ·
My Ladys Swamp
Hard Corner
Hustle
Dismal Swamp

Halfway ·
Hogwallow Flat Overlook ▲
Casanova ·
Big Ugly Run Trail ▲
Wolftown ·

Mole Hill

Lickinghole Creek

Cuckoo

Highcock Knob

Rustburg

Disputanta
Nutbush ·

Maggoty Creek

Tight Squeeze

Big End
House Hole

Mud · Lick

Motley ·

Matrimony Creek

Looney ·

Alls Cemetery □
Mechanicsburg

Bland ·
Tickle Pink Hollow
· Fries

Big Butt School

Little Town ·

· Lick Skillet
Hussy Mt. ▲

The Butt
The Suck

· Butts
Hash Cemetery □
Naked Run

Necessary Cemetery □

Virginians, a people of culture and refinement, have kept their outrageous places a secret. Visitor information centers direct tourists to famous attractions such as Colonial Williamsburg, Historic Jamestown, Appomattox, or the beautiful Shenandoah National Park. Virginians would like you to believe that they prefer a sedate tour of *My Ladys Swamp* to cavorting on the beaches at *Assawoman Bay.*

Begin your tour of outrageous Virginia places in the northern portion of the state. There you can look out over the countryside from *Hogwollow Flat Overlook.* Next go south to Elkton, and enjoy hiking along the *Big Ugly Run Trail.* Before traveling to southern Virginia, stop and tour the unrestored old homes in *House Hole,* west of Highway 220. The best adventures await you in southern Virginia, where you can be tickled pink at *Tickle Pink Hollow,* near Wythville.

Virginia cemeteries serve many functions. Tired of eating hash? You can bury it at *Hash Cemetery.* Your cheesecake can rest in peace at *Cheesecake Cemetery.* You can bury anything at *Alls Cemetery.* And there are no frivolous funerals at *Necessary Cemetery.*

Arguably the best vacation in Virginia is at *Disputanta.* Those seeking an unusual vacation experience should visit *Odd.* When a batter on the town's baseball team strikes out, he is of course the *Odd* man out. Beyond *Odd* is *Cuckoo.* The *Cuckoo* mayor and other *Cuckoo* officials wish to encourage *Cuckoo* tourism. *Nutbush* is obviously a competitor for the vacationer's time. While in *Looney,* you will need to obey *Looney* laws.

If you don't like *Odd, Nutbush, Cuckoo,* or *Looney,* you can vacation in *Ordinary,* Virginia. You can stay at an *Ordinary* hotel, eat at an *Ordinary* restaurant, and have *Ordinary* experiences. If *Ordinary* is too exciting, then a visit to *Bland* is a must. There you can enjoy a truly *Bland* vacation.

The very daring tourist can take the passion tour of Virgina. Speed by *Casanova* to *Wolftown.* Get to *Halfway,* via *Tight Squeeze.* Go on to *Hustle,* via *Hussy Mountain.* After *Hard Corner,* it is not too far to *High Cock Knob.* Then go to *Naked Run* on your way to *Matrimony Creek.*

It is well known that some males are breast men, and some males are leg men. However, in Virginia they are butt men. The state's butts make a suitable end for any vacation. There is *The Butt*, for those that have a special one in mind. For those that have more than one in mind, there is *Butts*. Men who value intellectual qualities as well as large rear ends head for *Big Butt School*. The more refined prefer *Big End*.

Other unusual and often overlooked places are *The Suck, Little Town, Frogstool, Mole Hill, Dismal Swamp, Lickinghole Creek, and* Maggoty Creek.

Washington

"The Evergreen State"

True Facts and Silly Stats

Population: 4,887,941
Area: 66,512 sq. mi.
Capital: Olympia
Largest City: Seattle
State Motto: My God, Is It Still Raining?
Climate: Great, if you're a mushroom
State Bird: Boeing Airplane
State Flower: Mildew
State Proverb: Soak in the West, Shrivel in the East
State Rain Forest: Olympic National Park
State Festival: The Pilgrimage of the Homeless to Seattle
Best Museum: Museum of Flight in Seattle
Major Tourist Attractions: Mount Rainier and Cascades National
   Park

Outrageous Tour Highlights

The state of Washington is divided into two distinct regions by the Cascade Mountains. To the west of the Cascades, the state has high rainfall and is covered by lush forest. The Olympic Peninsula, in the west, presents the chance to visit a temperate rain forest. To the east of the Cascades, the land is parched prairie.

Famous for its natural beauty, Washington also holds great delights for the outrageous sophisticate. There is no need to restrict your tour to Seattle, with its symphony, art center, and the Pacific Science Center. A solid, urban vacation can be had at

173

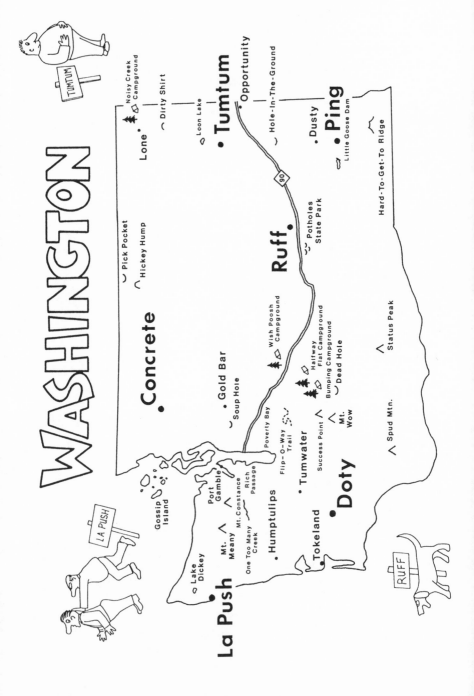

Concrete, on Highway 20. Enjoy the atmosphere at *Dusty*, on Highway 26, north of *Ping*. Savor the easygoing ways of *La Push*. And, watch the antics of the counterculture at *Tokeland*.

Washington has many parks, forests, and recreation areas. The most spectacular are Olympic National Park, Mount Rainier National Park, and North Cascades National Park. Less well known is *Potholes State Park*, the only park in America dedicated to preserving the worst in unrepaired roads. You can get away from the tourist crowds at *Hard-To-Get-To Ridge*. A visit to *Mount Meany*, after visiting *Hard-To-Get-To Ridge*, is for the indefatigable tourist. For an awe inspiring sight, visit *Mount Wow*. *Spud Mountain* is a must stop for those who don't count calories.

Many exciting camping possibilities present themselves at every turn in Washington. *Wish Poosh Camp Ground* offers tantalizing possibilities for those who wish for poosh. Get a good night's sleep under the stars at *Noisy Creek Camp Ground*. Try to get a halfway good tent site at *Halfway Flat Campground*. You will need to buy collision insurance before staying at *Bumping Campground*.

Raise your pulse rate in Washington by traveling from *Lake Dickey* to *Mount Constance*. For those who want to remember a passion filled visit to Washington, a visit to *Hickey Hump* is a must. But be forewarned, a visit to *Hickey Hump* is talked about on *Gossip Island*. Visitors to *Hickey Hump* need to be aware that it is near *Pick Pocket Basin*. Tourists also need to take care of themselves when visiting the *Ruff* area of Washington. A visitor can have a *Ruff* time near Interstate 90, in the south central region.

Washington is the state for the person on the way up. Leave *Poverty Bay* for *Rich Passage*, *Opportunity*, *Gold Bar*, and *Success Point*. You will reach *Status Peak*, if you don't go to *Port Gamble*, you can visit *Status Peak*. And finally, *Dirty Shirt* is on everyone's laundry list of things to see.

Other unusual, often overlooked places are *Flip-O-Way Trail*, *Soup Hole*, *Humptulips*, *One Too Many Creek*, and *Hole-In-The-Ground*.

West Virginia

"The Mountain State"

True Facts and Silly Stats

Population: 1,801,625
Area: 24,124 sq. mi.
Capital: Charleston
Largest City: Charleston
Old-Fashioned Town: Lewisburg
Topography: Hilly and Mountainous
State Flower: Big Rhododendron
State Bird: Cardinal
State Motto: How Should I Know What's on the Other Side of the Hill?
State Fossil: Coalosaurus
State Strip Show: Strip Coal Mining
Antique Military-Industrial Establishment: Harpers Ferry
Major Tourist Attraction: Monongahela National Forest

Outrageous Tour Highlights

West Virginia's mountains are an attraction for tourists from populous nearby states. Long white water rivers and forest covered mountains lure outdoor enthusiasts. The Monongahela National Forest offers excellent scenery. Historic Harpers Ferry preserves the site of John Brown's Raid. John Brown had intended to spark a slave rebellion. His efforts failed, and he was hung. The Harper's Ferry incident accelerated the nation's slide toward Civil War. Harpers Ferry was a major arms manufacturing site, and the historic buildings preserve the ancestor of the modern military-industrial establishment.

WEST VIRGINIA

PEE WEE

DROOP

Good Zoo

Maggoty Run

Cider Run

Scratchers Run

Bullet Run

Next • • The Jug

Drunkard Bottom

Chicken Run

Blandville

Nutter Fort

Peewee

Buck Shuck Run

Sully

Stumptown

Suck Lick Run

Looneyville

Shock

Bulltown

Cheat Mts.

Seldom Seen School

Gip •

Dingy

Crank Cemetery

Dink

Jumping Gut Run

Nitro • Tad

Booza-Boo Hollow

Mudsuck Branch

Scary School

Hell for Certain

Muck Cemetery

Mud

• Boomer

Bumblebee Run

Droop

Big Ugly Creek

ODD

Crum

He Hollow

Odd

War

Bozoo

Butt Cemetery

Known for its rural charms and rugged mountain vistas, West Virginia will captivate the imagination of any traveler. West Virginia has prided itself on a reputation as a refuge for eccentrism. Those seeking an unusual vacation will find it at *Odd*, West Virginia. Enjoy the spectacle of *Odd* men, *Odd* women, and *Odd* young people working for *Odd* businesses. Those too odd for *Odd*, go to *Looneyville*. See the defenses built to protect the eccentrics at *Nutter Fort*. Tour the homes of the many giants of industry and the arts who have come from *Peewee*.

If you want to go to *War*, West Virginia is for you. Remarkably, it is as easy to get out of this *War* as to get into it. Have a blast at *Boomer*. However, you may want to plan your visits to *Shock* and *Nitro* carefully. If you don't like *Shock*, *Boomer*, or *War*, and want peace and quiet, visit *Blandville*. If none of this appeals to you, you might want to stick to *Chicken Run*.

After a long journey, many travelers feel they have been through hell, but by visiting West Virginia, you will find *Hell for Certain*. It is between *Dingy* and *Droop* near Webster Springs.

Gip and the *Cheat Mountains* are questionable places to invest in real estate. And be sure you have the proper jogging shoes for *Suck Lick Run*, and soothing ointment for *Scratchers Run*.

Head to *Bozoo* for a truly sophisticated urbane experience. For sophisticated drinking there is *Mudsuck Brook*. If you want to get spooked, take the "creepy" tour of West Virginia which stops at *Muck Cemetery, Crank Cemetery, Booza-Boo Hollow, Scary School*, and *Maggoty Run*.

Other unusual, often overlooked places are *Buckshuck Run, Jumping Gut Run, Bullet Run, Drunkard Bottom*, and *The Jug*.

Wisconsin

"The Bong State"

True Facts and Silly Stats

Population: 4,906,745
Area: 54,424 sq. mi.
Capital: Madison
Largest City: Milwaukee
State Motto: We Produce Milk and Beer, But Don't Drink Them Together
Chief Products: Milk, Butter, and Cheese
Origin of State name: Indian word meaning, "Everything is being covered by cow pies"
State Artery Clogger: Cheese
State Artery Cleanser: Beer
Wisconsin Cultural Centers: Breweries
Famous Architecture: The House on the Rock (near Taliesin)
Major Tourist Attraction: Wisconsin Dells

Outrageous Tour Highlights

Wisconsin is a leading dairy state with pleasant farms and pine forests. The countryside is dotted with thousands of small sparkling lakes. The Wisconsin Dells, a geological wonderland of cliffs and gorges, are a popular tourist attraction.

Those wishing to savor the natural beauty of Wisconsin on an outrageous tour have a mecca in the *Bong State Recreation Area*. Some people may not know that Wisconsin is the *Bong State*. The recreational possibilities of bongs are better known.

The name "Wisconsin" is variously reported to be derived from an Indian word meaning *grassy place* or *gathering of the*

WISCONSIN

PIPE

Lake Two

One Buck
Lake

Ding
Dong
Creek

Lake One

One-Shoe
Lake

Popcorn Corners

One Man
Lake

Nudist Lake

Spread Eagle

Foo Lake

Fat Lake

Scat
Lake

Tipler

Yechout
Lake

Dump Lake

Fickle Lake

Potato Lake

Breed

Egg Harbor

Go-To-It Lake

Lousy
Creek

94

Chili

Embarrass

Penny
Lake

Speck Oats

Chickenbreast
Bluff

Rural

Pipe

Hustler

HUSTLER

Dilly

Hustler

End Park

Gross
Valley

Inch Church

Plugtown

Gompers Church

Fussville

BREED

90

Footville

Bong State
Recreation Area

waters. The reason for this rather large difference in meaning may depend on which particular Indian group early explorers were consulting. English speakers often missed nuances of meaning when recording Indian words. For example, it is known that the name of one Indian brave meant "One who is so mighty that even the (meer) sight of his horses strikes fear." The English translation of this man's name was "Afraid of His Horses." Given the extent to which Indian names were mistranslated, it is possible that when Indians were heard saying "Ouisconsin" or "Mesconsing," they were refering to the bong recreation area.

A tourist wishing to enjoy the bucolic wonder of Wisconsin's countryside must visit *Rural,* on scenic Highway 22. Other bucolic communities are *Speck Oats* and *Plugtown.* If you would rather explore urban life with a walking tour, there is *Footville,* on Highway 11. You can experience urban strife at *Fussville,* north of Milwaukee. And view a religious congregation at *Inch Church.*

The gastronomic extravaganza that is Wisconsin can be savored at *Chili, Potatoe Lake,* and *Egg Harbor.* This generally exhausts the items on most menus in the state. Those seeking the thrills of Wisconsin vice should visit *Nudist Lake, Hustler,* and *Spread Eagle.*

Wisconsin is known for its remarkable lakes. *Penny Lake* is for the economical tourist. *One Buck Lake* is for the more affluent. *Dump Lake* doesn't sound very nice, but *Scat Lake* sounds even worse, but for the outrageous traveler they are both musts.

It has been reported that there are more overweight people in Wisconsin than in any other state. But this is natural since the state has obese topographic features such as *Fat Lake,* not far from *Popcorn Corners.* Specialized lake tours include *One Man Lake, Fickle Lake,* and *One-Shoe Lake.*

Other unusual, often overlooked places to see are *Ding Dong Creek, Go-to-it-Lake, Chickenbreast Bluff, Foo Lake,* and *Lousy Creek.*

Wyoming

"The Equality State"

True Facts and Silly Stats

Population: 455,975
Area: 96,988 sq. mi.
Capital: Cheyenne
Largest City: Cheyenne
State Bird: Meadowlark
State Motto: Why Do They Say CowBOYS, But SheepMEN?
State Wisdom: Bowlegged cowboys are sexy
State Proverb: Let the tourists pet the buffalo, our health care
    system needs the business
State's Source of Hot Running Water: Old Faithful
Most Spectacular Mountain Range: The Grand Tetons
Major Tourist Attraction: Yellowstone National Park

Outrageous Tour Highlights

Wyoming is a state where the Great Plains meet the Rocky Mountains. The name, Wyoming, is from an Indian word believed to mean either "large prairie place" or "alternating mountains and valleys." Whether it is mountains, valleys, or prairies, Wyoming's natural wonders make it an awe inspiring tourist bonanza. Out-of-state visitors spend approximately 1.5 billion dollars a year in Wyoming. Yellowstone Park alone has almost three million visitors. The number of visitors to Yellowstone Park each year is more than six times the permanent number of residents of the entire state. There have been concerns that parks in Wyoming, like Yellowstone and Grand Teton, are overcrowded. Campsites fill up early. Sometimes

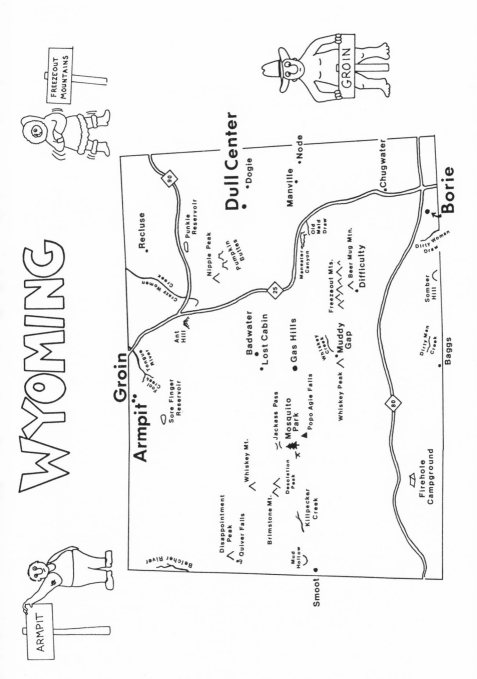

visitors in their cars line up at the camp entrances early in the morning in order to get the first available campsites. This can leave tourists who come later in the day without a place to pitch their tents or hook up their RV's.

In order to alleviate tourist pressure on the National Parks, we would like to point out some other colorful places in Wyoming that are not overcrowded. *Lost Cabin* is available, if you can find it. (We'll give you a hint, it's north of Highway 20/26, between Casper and Shoshoni.) Few tourists frequent *Mosquito Park* near *Wind River.* You can also get away from the crowds at *Mud Hollow,* near *Smoot,* and at *Killpecker Creek* not too far from *Halfway.*

Are you interested in boating on one of Wyoming's beautiful lakes, but afraid of the crowds? Instead of towing your boat to Jackson and Jenny Lakes beneath the Grand Tetons, head for *Punkie Reservoir* near Gillette in the northeast portion of the state. If, by chance, there are too many people at *Punkie,* try *Sore Finger Reservoir* between Greybull and Cody.

Other places not taxed by tourists are *Disappointment Peak* and *Somber Hill.* Motel rooms are usually available at *Difficulty* south of the *Freezeout Mountains.* A place in Wyoming that is avoided by most tourists is *Maneater Canyon* near Douglas. And, nightclubs are rarely crowded at *Dull Center* or *Borie.* Bring your own drinks and fill up at the *Whiskey* and *Beer Mug Mountain* campgrounds. Finally, *Recluse* near Spotted Horse on Highway 14/16 is the ideal getaway.

Wyoming is known as the "equal rights" state, because it was in Wyoming Territory that women first won the right to vote in the U.S. True to its nickname, Wyoming established equality in all things, even in dirty person place-names. This is evidenced by the existence of *Dirty Man Creek* and *Dirty Woman Draw* in the state.

Other unusual places are *Nipple Peak, Jackass Pass, Pumpkin Buttes,* and *Ant Hill.*

The Provinces and Territories of Canada

Alberta

"The Dinosaur Province"

True Facts and Silly Stats

Population: 2,237,724
Area: 255,285 sq. mi.
Capital: Edmonton
Largest City: Calgary
Province Motto: Like Hell We'll Share Our Oil Wells
Province Food: Beef (cold cuts)
Province Rush Hour: Calgary Stampede
Province Fossil: Oilosaurus
Biggest Attractions: Dinosaur skeletons at the Royal Tyrrell
     Museum of Palaeontology near Drumheller
Major Tourist Attractions: Banff and Jasper National Parks

Outrageous Tour Highlights

One of the world's most unforgettable traveling experiences is Alberta, Canada. Take time to enjoy Alberta's extraordinary scenery. The majesty and beauty of the Canadian Rockies can best be appreciated from this province. Numerous spectacular national parks are found in Alberta, including Jasper, Banff, Yoho, and Kootenay. The national parks are well maintained and easy to access. Calgary is the chief urban attraction. The city has the fine Glenbow Museum which has exhibits on the Canadian West. Calgary is also the site of a spectacular annual rodeo, known as the Calgary Stampede.

Enjoy Alberta, but don't be surprised if an outrageous tour of Alberta's places leads you to embarrassment. Few visitors upon arrival know that Alberta is "the land of double embar-

187

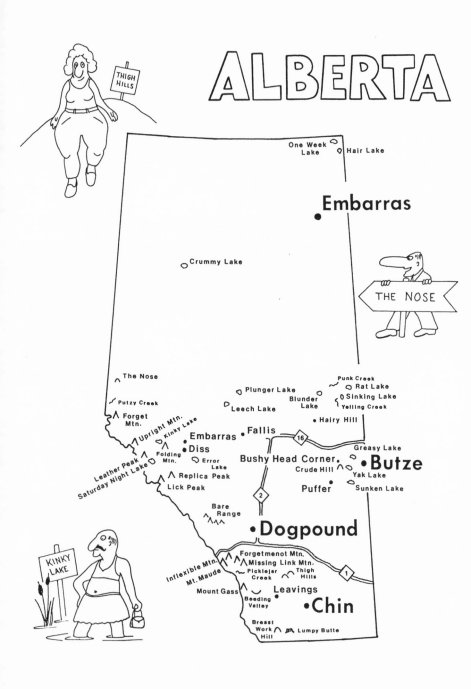

ALBERTA

THIGH HILLS

One Week Lake

Hair Lake

• Embarras

Crummy Lake

THE NOSE

The Nose

Putzy Creek

Plunger Lake

Punk Creek

Rat Lake

Blunder Lake

Sinking Lake

Leech Lake

Yelling Creek

Forget Mtn.

Upright Mtn.

Kinky Lake

Embarras

• Fallis

Hairy Hill

16

• Diss

Leather Peak

Folding Mtn.

Error Lake

Bushy Head Corner

Greasy Lake

• Butze

Saturday Night Lake

Crude Hill

Yak Lake

Replica Peak

Puffer

Sunken Lake

Lick Peak

2

Bare Range

• Dogpound

KINKY LAKE

Forgetmenot Mtn.

Missing Link Mtn.

Inflexible Mtn.

Picklejar Creek

Thigh Hills

1

Mt. Maude

Mount Gass

Leavings

Beeding Valley

• Chin

Breast Work Hill

Lumpy Butte

rassment." There is an *Embarras* in the northeast of the province, and an *Embarras* in the southwest as well. The visitor can easily comprehend one of the sources of local embarrassment after viewing topography at *Thigh Hills*, north of Lethbridge. Family tours wishing to avoid embarrassment, should steer clear of *Breeding Valley*, in the southwest corner of the province. Also avoid *Breast Work Hill*, near *Lumpy Butte* in the south and *Bare Range*, northwest of Calgary. Single men may be embarrassed by picking up dates at *Dogpound*. At *Kinky Lake* and *Leather Peak* west of *Fallis*, you will see further reason for embarrassment. At *Fallis*, they know what it is, but they just can't spell it. In any event, you should avoid the place during hard times.

There is no need for the visitor to avoid *Crude Hill*, because from its summit you can see a more refined topography. Balance your sightseeing excursion to *Replica Peak* in Jasper National Park by seeking out an authentic one. You may want to postpone a visit to *Sunken Lake*, until after they've raised it above water. However, be sure to visit *Sinking Lake*, before it goes under water. *Blunder Lake* and *Error Lake* have been publicly acknowledged as mistakes. However, do see *Upright Mountain* in Jasper National Park, which exhibits the basic essence of a vertical landmass. *Inflexible Mountain* west of Calgary is not a place for those who like to see mountains flex. However, those who like to fold mountains will enjoy the *Folding Mountain*, near Highway 16, west of Edmonton.

Ultimately, it would seem Albertans have trouble making up their minds, as witnessed by the existence of *Forget Mountain* and *Forgetmenot Mountain*. And there is always the memorable *Missing Link Mountain*, southwest of Calgary.

Visit *Crummy Lake* in the north central portion of the province if you want, but you can probably find a better one. For the best in temporary lakes, visit *One Week Lake*, in the northeast corner of the province. *Leech Lake*, northwest of Edmonton, is one lake to which any visitor will form an attachment. Also north of Edmonton is *Saturday Night Lake*, a happening place to be sure.

We recommend that you pick *The Nose,* north of Grand Cache, as one of your anatomical destinations. If *The Nose* is not enough to satisfy your desire to visit body parts, you can drop down to see *Chin,* east of Lethbridge. If you go down any further, you'll reach *Butze,* which is best viewed in the moonlight.

Other unusual and often overlooked places to visit are *Punk Creek, Putzy Creek, Mount Gass, Leavings,* and *Bushy Head Corner.*

British Columbia

"The Mountain Province"

True Facts and Silly Stats

Population: 2,744,467 plus China
Area: 366,255 sq. mi.
Capital: Victoria
Largest City: Vancouver
Province Motto: Cool and Clammy Suits Me Just Dandy
First Tourist: Sir Francis Drake
Best Unspoiled Scenery: The Kootenays
Abundant Victorian Architecture: Nelson
Best Museum: Museum of Anthropology, Vancouver
Major Tourist Attractions: Victoria, Crystal, and Butchart
    Gardens
Major Sexual Activity: Spawning Salmon

Outrageous Tour Highlights

British Columbia has a vast range of exceptionally spectacular scenery. High rainfall over much of British Columbia has created a lush environment including areas of rainforest. The province contains a remarkable diversity of types of recreation. Opportunities to fish, canoe, hike, ski, and sail abound. Because of its natural setting, Vancouver is one of the world's most beautiful cities. The Museum of Anthropology, on the University of British Columbia campus in Vancouver, has the finest collection of native northwest coast art in North America.

British Columbia is a land of infinite beauty, carved by ancient glaciers. A few of these glaciers are still hanging around to inspire awe in the traveler. *Miserable Glacier,* however, may not be the example you want to see. *Wrong Glacier* has been publicly acknowledged as a mistake. *OK Glacier* is better. Have an adrenalin raising tour of *Assault Glacier,* the only known

BRITISH COLUMBIA

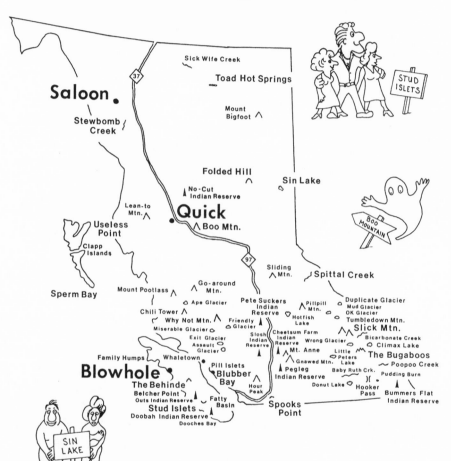

Sick Wife Creek

Toad Hot Springs

STUD ISLETS

Saloon .

Stewbomb Creek

Mount Bigfoot ∧

Folded Hill ∧

Sin Lake ○

Mount Bigfoot

No-Cut Indian Reserve ∧

Lean-to Mtn. ∧

Quick

Useless Point

∧ Boo Mtn.

BOO MOUNTAIN

Clapp Islands

Sliding ∧ Mtn.

Sperm Bay

Mount Pootlass ∧

Go-around ∧ Mtn.

Spittal Creek

Duplicate Glacier

Mud Glacier

Pete Suckers Indian Reserve

Pillpill Mtn.

OK Glacier

Tumbledown Mtn.

Chili Tower ⌒

∧ Ape Glacier

Why Not Mtn. ∧

Friendly ○ Glacier

Hotfish Lake

Slick Mtn.

Miserable Glacier ○

Slosh Indian Reserve

Cheetsum Farm Indian Reserve

Wrong Glacier

Bicarbonate Creek

Exit Glacier

○ Climax Lake

Assault Glacier ○

Little ∧ Peters Lake

Family Humps ⌐

Whaletown

▲ Mt. Anne

The Bugaboos

Blowhole ●

Pill Islets

∧ Gnawed Mtn.

~ Poopoo Creek

Blubber Bay

Pegleg Indian Reserve

Baby Ruth Crk.

Pudding Burn

The Behinde

Hour Peak

Donut Lake ○

)(Hooker Pass

▲ Bummers Flat

Belcher Point ⌐

Outs Indian Reserve

Stud Islets ▲

Fatty Basin

Spooks Point

Indian Reserve

Doobah Indian Reserve

Dooches Bay

SIN LAKE

attack glacier to defend a wilderness area. After minimizing the environmental impact of your camping at *Attack Glacier,* you will be relieved to know that there is a spare of *Duplicate Glacier.* You probably won't care whether or not there is a spare of *Mud Glacier,* but for those frightened of ice, there is *Friendly Glacier.* Finally, those wanting to get away from it all should visit *Exit Glacier.*

The mountains of British Columbia are a favorite of tourists. Unfortunately they have been visited so much, they are getting run down. Don't visit *Tumbledown Mountain* until the Canadian government appropriates money to prop it up. Additional topographic improvement is needed at *Lean-to Mountain.* Note to the traveler, visiting time is limited at *Hour Peak.* And if you don't like detours, avoid *Go-around Mountain.*

Those who ask why men scale the high peaks get their answer at *Why Not Mountain.* If you enjoy the thrills and spills of sliding down a mountain, try *Slick Mountain* or *Sliding Mountain.* *Folded Hill* is for tidy travelers. After a visit to *Sick Wife Creek,* you had better head to *Pill Islets.* We don't know how much of *Pill Islets* you can take, but you can get twice as much at *Pillpill Mountain.*

No trip to this province is complete without a visit to *Saloon.* On Sunday, visit the remarkable *Saloon* church, where the services emphasize communion.

The colorful American Indians of British Columbia can be found on a number of remarkable Indian reservations. *Pegleg Indian Reserve* was established more than a century ago for Indian pirates. The *Outs Indian Reserve* is clearly not for the "ins." You'll be safe from knife wounds at *No-Cut Indian Reserve.* The *Slosh Indian Reserve* is not to imply that the Indians there are sloshed. *Bummers Flat Indian Reserve* may be a bummer, but at least it is level. Be sure to count your produce at *Cheetsum's Farm Indian Reserve.* *Pete Suckers Indian Reserve* is a fearsome place if your name happens to be Pete.

British Columbians are renowned for big appetites. This becomes obvious by a visit to *Gnawed Mountain.* The outrageous gastronomic tour stops at *Baby Ruth Creek, Donut*

Lake, and *Fatty Basin.* Continuing on to *Chili Tower, Stewbomb Creek,* and *Pudding Burn,* then to the penultimate destination, *Belcher Point,* which is traditionally followed by a cruise down *Bicarbonate Creek.*

For the scary tour it's on to *Boo Mountain,* next stop is the *Spooks Point,* then finally *The Bugaboos.*

The best tour in British Columbia is *Quick.* The teachers in town have the advantage of *Quick* students. You can buy *Quick* sand at the local sand and gravel company. The town and its cemetery are known as the *Quick* and the dead, while local males are known as the *Quick* in bed.

With so many outstanding sights, it is important to plan your itinerary carefully. You wouldn't want to miss anything. If you must cut your vacation short, we suggest you save time by avoiding *Useless Point.*

The virility of British Columbians has never been challenged, in fact it has never been brought up. The well endowed vacation at *Stud Islets,* others stay at *Little Peters Lake.* Cruise *Sin Lake* and reach *Sperm Bay* and the unforgettable *Climax Lake.* You may even find yourself anchored at *Clapp Islands.* The locals, always a people of sophisticated discernment, advise that it is better to go to *Mount Anne* than to *Mount Bigfoot.* Upon reaching the end of your vacation in British Columbia, you will discover that *Blowhole* is embarrassingly near *The Behinde.*

Other unusual and often overlooked places are *Poopoo Creek, Spittal Creek, Mount Pootlass,* and *Dooches Bay*

Manitoba

"The Lake Province"

True Facts and Silly Stats

Population: 1,026,241
Area: 251,000 sq. mi.
Capital: Winnipeg
Largest City: Winnipeg
Province Motto: We Drive at Night, When the View Is More
    Spectacular
Province Bird: Blackfly
Province Cologne: Insect Repellent
Best Museum: Manitoba Museum of Man and Nature, Winnipeg
Largest Lake: Lake Winnipeg
Major Town With Polar Bears in the City Park: Churchill
Major Tourist Attraction: Riding Mountain National Park

Outrageous Tour Highlights

Manitoba, the land of sparkling lakes, beckons the tourist to escape the summer heat in its cool northern waters. The lakes are the result of ancient glaciers that altered drainages during the Ice Age. The numerous lakes offer many recreational opportunities for fishing and canoeing. The area was not heavily settled by pioneers until the turn of the century, leaving less time for the natural wonders to be affected by development. So numerous are Manitoba's lakes that the province has a lake for virtually everyone. A host of colorful place-names also provide a variety of outrageous tour possibilities.

Tallish tourists can revel at the *Longish Lakes*, east of Lake Winnipeg. The petite enjoy *Shorty Lake*, in the northwestern

195

MANITOBA

BLADDER RAPIDS

Belcher

Yellow Water River

Oldman River

Lost Moose Creek

Fly Lake

End Lake

In Lake Swede Lake
Shorty Lake Pole Lake
Lasthope Lake

Atomic Lake

Cuddle Lake

Found Lake
Love Lake Puffy Lake
Lost Frog Lake
Buzz Lake

Drinking Lake
Leech Lake

Button

Bladder Rapids

Drunken Lake

Whiskey Jack Landing

Ant Lake

Winking Point

Strip Rapids

Okay Island

Flin Flon

Naked Bay

Finger

Streak Lake

SHORTIE LAKE

10

Dancing Point

Goodwater Lake

Skin Lake

Wrong Lake

Stag Lake

Longish Lakes

Lost Lake
Wine Lake

Snake Lake

The Halfway
Magnet

Ebb and Flow Lake

Shesheep Lake

DRUNKEN LAKE

Spider Lake

Grosse Isle Milkhouse **Decimal**

Tuxedo Contour

1

Dipples Moosenose

Pansy Moodie

Shoofly Lake

portion of the Province. Trend setters head for *In Lake,* not far from *Shorty Lake.* Those who like to search, can look for *Lost Lake.* Those who don't, look for *Found Lake,* northeast of *Flin Flon.* Those who end up at the *Wrong Lake* in Manitoba can try again at *Lasthope Lake.* Visit *Swede Lake,* and if you don't like its ethnic charm, you can head for nearby *Pole Lake.*

Those in search of a drinking vacation will want to visit *Whiskey Jack Landing.* If you don't stop at *Drinking Lake,* you may end up at *Drunken Lake.* After a long swim in *Wine Lake,* west of Highway 10, you'll be ready for *Buzz Lake.* Be sure to have a beer at the *Belcher Bar* on your way to Churchill. After visiting the bar, you'll feel the need to stop by *Bladder Rapids* on the Nelson River. From there it is not too far to *Yellow Water River.* Thankfully, *Yellow Water River* does not drain into *Goodwater Lake.*

Although the winters are cold enough in Manitoba to freeze over the lakes, passions always run hot. The adventurous visitor can go from *Winking Point* and *Okay Island* in the east to the *Strip Rapids,* on the Stevenson River. Such a bold itinerary moves on from *Strip Rapids* to *Streak Lake* and ends up in *Naked Bay.* For the shy, there is *Cuddle Lake,* while the experienced traveler will dive right into *Skin Lake.*

Tourists can come and go at wonderful *Ebb and Flow Lake* near Shergrove. No tourist will want to miss *The Halfway* settlement on the east shore of the Fisher River. Homes in the town are, of course, known as *The Halfway* houses. The formal tourist can stay at *Tuxedo,* southwest of Winnipeg. However, some people may be attracted to *Magnet.* When you visit *Button,* you will discover that any excavation is a *Button* hole. People who don't like the place refer to it as *the Button* hole. Most visitors end their visit to Manitoba at *End Lake.*

Additional unusual and often overlooked places to see are *Leech Lake, Puffy Lake,* and *Lost Moose Creek.*

New Brunswick

"The Land of Rugged People"

True Facts and Silly Stats

Population: 696,403
Area: 28,354 sq. mi.
Capital: Fredericton
Largest City: Saint John
Native People: Micmac and Malicites
Economy: Lumbering, agriculture, and fishing
Climate: Winter will definitely kill tomatoes
Interior: Largely uninhabited
Province Motto: We Are Like Maine, But More So
Major Tourist Attraction: Fundy National Park

Outrageous Tour Highlights

The citizens of New Brunswick have a rugged character that has arisen from their history. New Brunswick was largely settled by people fleeing persecution such as British loyalists fleeing the newly independent United States and French-speaking Acadians. The industries the pioneers worked were as rugged as their character; these included logging, ship building, fishing, and mining.

Perhaps because of their rugged nature, the people of New Brunswick have been great admirers of rocks. New Brunswick has a plethora of colorful names for rocks. For example, there is *Boring Stone,* south of St. Stephen. *Boring Stone*'s name was evidently derived by comparing it to other New Brunswick rocks that are the life of the party. *Plumper Rock,* southwest of Saint John, apparently contrasts with the anorexic rocks that litter the

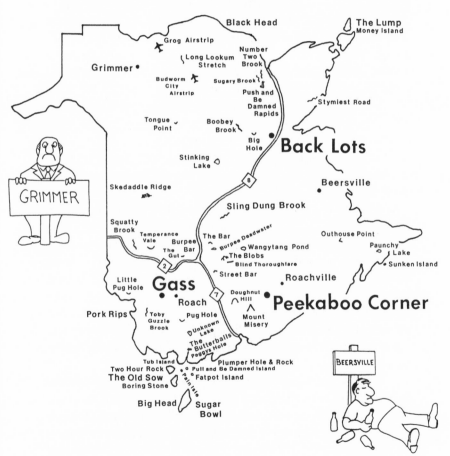

landscape in other places. People who mistakenly believe in the permanence of stone should visit *Two Hour Rock*, south of St. Stephen.

New Brunswick is noted for its sparkling waters, where the aficionado of pristine nature can splash about in cool, clear streams. But rugged individuals do not utilize the facilities that most tourists have become accustomed to. For example, there is the case of *Number Two Brook*. You can well imagine what the locals do at *Number Two Brook*. If you have any doubts about what they do, you should visit *Squatty Brook*. At least the local people have running water in their toilet facilities. All of this seems wholesome compared to what goes on at *Slingdung Brook*. We would like to point out *Outhouse Point* for travelers wishing to spare the local waterways.

The rugged residents of New Brunswick are not squeamish about the water they drink. Nevertheless, *Burpee Deadwater* is not the place to start a business exporting bottled water. Nor is *Stinking Lake* ideal for such an enterprise. The distinctive taste of *Wanytang Pond* water, however, might attract customers from far and wide.

No visit to New Brunswick is complete without a trip to *Grimmer*. There you can see the *Grimmer* church, with the *Grimmer* parishioners, and *Grimmer* minister. The *Grimmer* celebrations of the town's people are remarkable, and if you are there over the holidays you can celebrate a *Grimmer* Christmas and a *Grimmer* New Year.

New Brunswick is justly famous as a rugged vacation wonderland. Visit the island designed especially for dentists at *Pain Isle*. For mountain climbing dentists, there is *Mount Misery*. And doctors may want to vacation on *Money Island*.

The people of the province are proud of the physiques they have built by a lifetime of good eating. This can clearly be seen at *The Butterballs* and *Pork Rips*. The well fed and middle aged splash about in *Paunchy Lake,* while the really obese vacation on *Tub Island,* near St. Stephen, or *Fat Pot Island*. Since it's easy to gain weight at *Sugar Bowl, Sugary Brook,* and *Doughnut Hill,* we suggest a traveler's itinerary include a few days at *The Blobs* spa, east of Fredericton.

New Brunswick is not only known for its food, but also its drink. After guzzling your fill at *Beersville,* you should head directly for *Burpee Bar,* where the effects will not be noticed. Visit the brook, *Toby Guzzle,* named in commemoration of the province's most beloved wino. Those with a generic thirst can visit *The Bar,* while those who don't mind the traffic can drink at *Street Bar.* A long stay at *Temperance Vale* is recommended after such a bar crawling tour.

The anatomical tour of New Brunswick is one of the province's greatest spectacles. Visit local egotists at *Big Head,* off the southern coast, and the gossipers at *Tongue Point.* Take a cruise down the channel known as *The Gut,* and all on board will be known as people who passed through *The Gut.* Stay awhile and learn the ins and outs of *Peggy's Hole,* southwest of Saint John. Voyeurs will want to visit *Peekaboo Corner* and *Long Lookum Stretch,* and definitely must spend time at *Boobey Brook,* not far from Newcastle.

New Brunswick has rugged accommodations. While at *Roach,* you can stay at the *Roach* motel. In the north, watch the thrilling takeoffs and landings at *Budworm City Airstrip,* the only budworm airport in the world. Another specialty airport is *Grog Airstrip.*

As you may have guessed, the rugged people of New Brunswick are not afraid of the unusual. You can see sights coming and going at the expense of your soul at *Push and Be Damned* and *Pull and Be Damned.*

Nor do the rugged individuals of the province flinch at driving under any conditions. Keep your white cane pointing out the car window for safety's sake when you speed down *Blind Thoroughfare.* Try not to be stopped by *Stymiest Road.* At *Skedaddle Ridge,* bid a fond farewell to New Brunswick.

Other unusual, often overlooked places are *The Old Sow, Unknown Lake, Little Pug Hole, The Lump, Big Hole,* and *Back Lots.*

Newfoundland

"The Tickle Province"

True Facts and Silly Stats

Population: 567,681
Area: 156,185 sq. mi.
Capital: St. John's
Largest City: St. John's
Province Motto: We Have Fought Over Cod
Native People: Beothuk
Early Explorer: John Cabot in 1497
Major Industry: Fishing for Cod
Provincal Upper Crust: Codocracy
Best Fishing: Grand Banks
Major Tourist Attraction: Seal, whale, and iceberg watching

Outrageous Tour Highlights

Newfoundland has picturesque fishing villages, magnificent rugged coasts, spectacular fiords, high mountains, white water rivers, sparkling lakes, and vast interior forests. The first known European settlement in the New World occurred at L'Anse aux Meadows with the establishment of a Viking colony in the eleventh century. Although this early Norse colony failed, its traces remain as an archaeological site.

If you are looking for a laugh, the natives of Newfoundland will give you one at *The Tickle*. For grim titillation, there is *Cut Throat Tickle*. Laughs for senior citizens are available at *Old Island Tickle*. Get tickled with a white cane at *Blind Tickle*. See how familiar the sailors get at *Captain Jack's Tickle*. For those

NEWFOUNDLAND

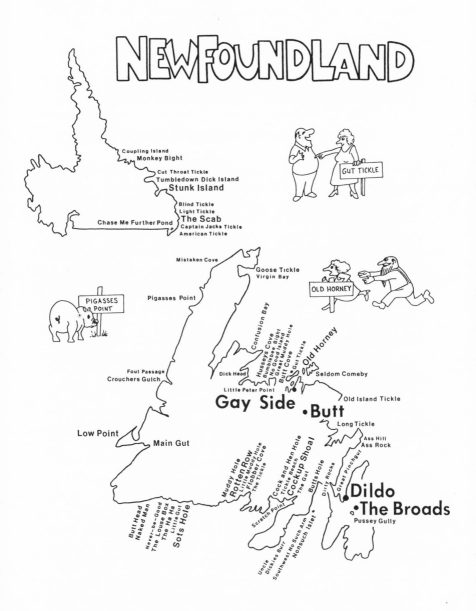

getting tickled too much, there is *Light Tickle,* and for those wanting more, there is *Long Tickle.* Those who want to be tickled by a Yankee can go to *American Tickle.* For tummy ticklers there is *Gut Tickle,* an experience surpassed only by *Goose Tickle.* Enjoy the sun, the surf, and the titillation at *Tickle Beach.* All these tickles undoubtedly explain *The Ha Ha.*

Avoid the primitive restroom facilities at *Crouchers Gulch.* There is no need to avoid *Stunk Island,* because the use of the past tense indicates it no longer stinks.

Many landmarks are named after prominent politicians in Newfoundland, such as *Ass Hill, Dick Head* and *Butt Head.* Visit the point where you can view the westward ends of eastward moving pigs, at *Pigasses Point.* It would seem that the fine people of New Foundland have a special fondness for buttocks. The following point will be of great interest to the outrageous traveller with a penchant for butts of all kinds, including: the generic *Butts,* the localized *Butts Cove, Ass Rock,* and the ever popular *Butts Hole.*

Newfoundland has many good points. But it would seem places like *Foul Passage, Rotten Row,* and *No Good Island* are not among them. In fact, the *Low Point* of your Canadian vacation awaits you in Newfoundland. Those seeking sophistication and "la dolce vita" will flock to *Muddy Hole.* If that is too much for you, there is *Little Muddy Hole.* If that is not enough, there is *Great Muddy Hole.* Share a depression with barnyard fowl at *Cock and Hen Hole.*

It's not always easy to find your way around this province. For example, *Southwest No Such Arm* is located near *Nonsuch Inlet.* Many travelers have lost their direction at *Confusion Bay* and also *Mistaken Cove.*

Visit *Dildo*, a vibrant but somewhat artificial community. Perhaps there is a need for a *Dildo* in this province, considering the presence of *Troubledown Dick Island* and *Little Peter Point.* Meet interesting women at *Chase Me Further Pond* and *Never-be-Good Shoal.* A Stay at *Old Horney* will lead to *Cockup*

Shoal and *Pussys Gully.* Those who anchor at *Hussy Cove* will never go back to *Virgin Bay.*

Other unusual, often overlooked places are *Uncle Dickies Burr, Dirty Rocks, Monkey Bight, Bumblebee Bight,* and *Flobber Cove.*

Northwest Territories

"The Frontier"

True Facts and Silly Stats

Population: 35 Eskimos, 12 Indians, and Santa Claus
Area: 1,271,442 sq. mi.
Capital: Yellowknife
Climate: Compares favorably to the North Pole
Highway System: 1 mile of road for every 1,800 square miles
Territorial Tree: Christmas Tree
Territorial Man of the Year: The Abominable Snowman
Sign of Winter Approaching: Men grow more hair on their
     chests
Favorite Winter Activity: Hibernation
Major Tourist Attractions: Wildlife and Aurora Borealis (North-
     ern Lights)

Outrageous Tour Highlights

The Northwest Territories is a vast area making up approximately a third of Canada's landmass. There are very few people
living there, and half of those who do, live in the vicinity of the
capital, Yellowknife. There are only a few roads and they are
restricted to the western and southern edges of the region.
Visitors come to this distant territory primarily to fish, hunt,
canoe, or see the pristine scenery. Because travel is so difficult,
the tourist should very carefully choose an itinerary.

The Northwest Territories have many good "points."
However, *Lousy Point* is not one of them. Drive carefully or you

NORTHWEST TERRITORIES

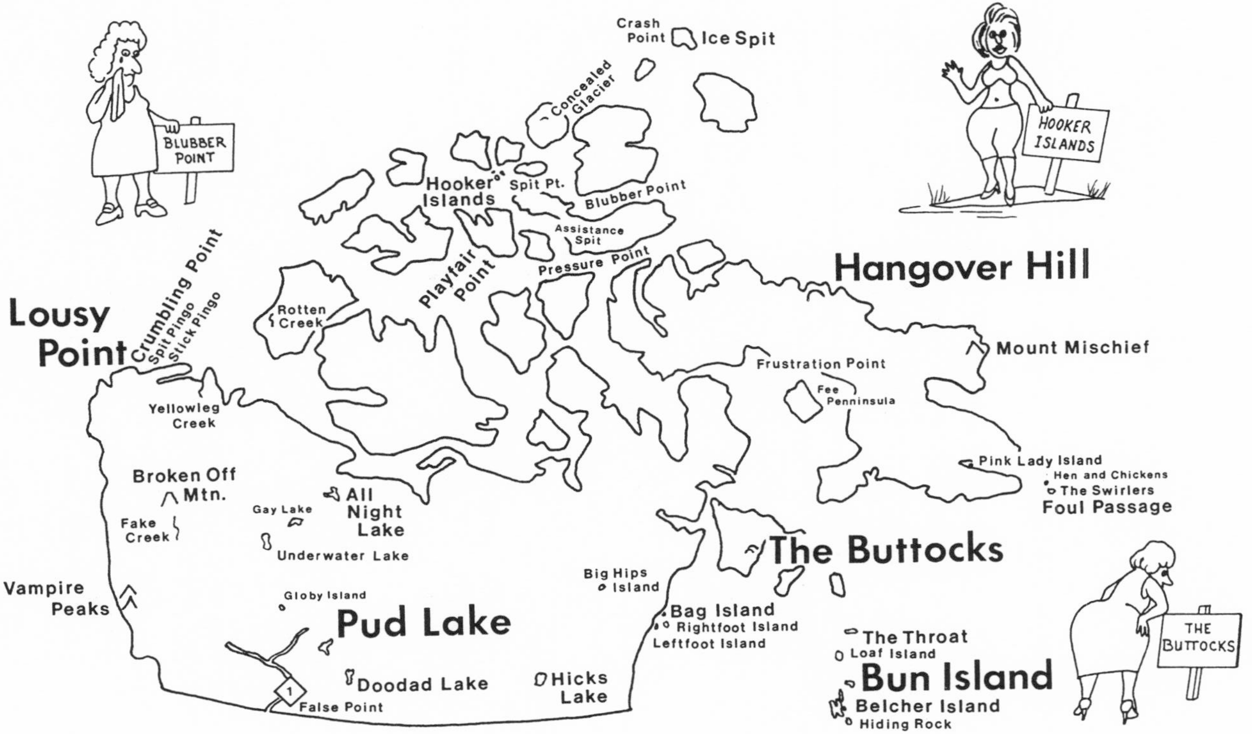

will likely run into *Crash Point*. If you get too much of *Pressure Point*, you may go to *Crumbling Point*. When you reach *Frustration Point*, you may be reduced to tears, in which case you have reacher *Blubber Point*.

The numerous unspoiled lakes that dot the region are a major drawing card. However, we recommend that fishermen avoid *Fake Creek* and instead search for a real one. Fishermen who have the urge to fish at night should head for *All Night Lake* where the place is open 24 hours a day, and does not close at 8:00 P.M. like the rest of the lakes in the Northwest Territories. Catch your limit in doodads, at *Doodad Lake*. Bring scuba gear if you want to fish at *Underwater Lake*. The scenery is unspoiled because few people have found *Underwater Lake,* probably because they have not thought to look underwater.

There are many magnificent glaciers in the Northwest Territories. Therefore, we suggest that you skip *Concealed Glacier* and sightsee where glaciers are more visible. It is legal in Canada to carry a concealed glacier, but you must be over 21 and have a license.

Rock hounds can spend an interesting afternoon looking for *Hiding Rock*. Or you can go see *Brokenoff Mountain* if you want, but you might as well visit an intact one. If you want to see some mountains that really suck, visit *Vampire Peaks*. Trouble-makers can scale *Mount Mischief*. The discerning traveler can watch the most spectacular moonrise in Canada, at *The Buttocks*.

The Buttocks is a major landmark in the anatomical geography of the far North. After *The Buttocks, Bun Island* is redundant. In this part of Canada, everyone goes for *The Throat*. If you get off on the right foot in the morning, you can go to *Rightfoot Islet*. If not, you can go to *Leftfoot Islet*.

The Northwest Territories are famous for spits. If you like to chew tobacco, there is *Spit Point*. Novices can get help in expectoration at *Assistance Spit*. If you like chewing cold tobacco, there is *Ice Spit*.

And finally, an added treat. Visit *Fee Peninsula* for the only known peninsula with a cover charge.

Some other unusual, often overlooked places to visit are *Globy Island, Hangover Hill, Yellowleg Creek, Spit Pingo,* and *Rotten Creek.*

Nova Scotia

"The Bluenose Province"

True Facts and Silly Stats

Population: 847,442
Area: 21,425 sq. mi.
Capital: Halifax
Largest City: Halifax
Province Motto: We Stayed, Even If the Vikings Wouldn't
Most Famous Export: Cajuns to Louisiana
Maritime Business: Fishing
Interior Business: Lumbering
Native People: Algonkians
Major Tourist Attraction: Kejimkujik National Park

Outrageous Tour Highlights

Nova Scotia, or "New Scotland," offers the visitor a remarkable panorama of charming fishing villages, forests, and lakes. Colonists of Nova Scotia came to be known as "bluenoses" because of the harsh north Atlantic climate they endured. Although Nova Scotia is noted for its scenic coastal beauty, a relaxed ambiance is also an attraction. Most visitors tour the picturesque fishing villages and lighthouses of the coast. The ultimate in a relaxed vacation is available in Nova Scotia for the connoisseur of outrageous places.

The departure point for a great sloth tour of Nova Scotia is *Land of Laziness Lake* north of Halifax. The tour spends several days at *Land of Laziness Lake,* where vacationers forget their hectic and harried workday lives. The lakefront cottages have

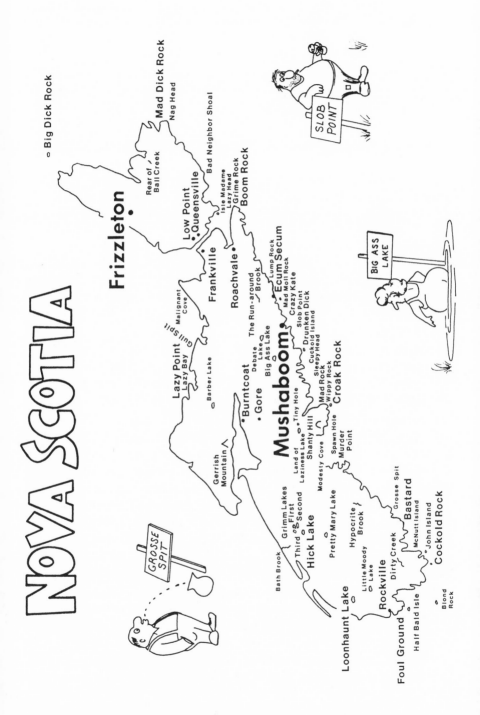

permanent "do not disturb" signs on the doors. Energetic tourists, who have trouble relaxing, can take an optional afternoon excursion to see Nova Scotia's exciting *Tiny Hole* not far from the lake. Tour buses, equipped with bunk beds, take the traveler in comfort to *Lazy Bay,* and then *Lazy Point,* on the north coast. Since most tourists on the sloth tour do not get off the buses to see the points of interest, the tour loops to the south to take in *Lazy Head* at Chedabucto Bay. The quiet ambiance of the tour is occasionally disrupted at *Lazy Head* by the booming of nearby *Boom Rock.* Ear plugs are a must for the well prepared traveler. The sloth tour ends at *Sleepy Head,* where tour guides carry the tired travelers to waiting taxis which then slowly drive to the Halifax airport for night flights home.

Another popular outrageous tour of Nova Scotia is the famous "rock tour." Nova Scotia has some of North America's most fascinating rocks. Two of the most notable are *Big Dick Rock* and *Mad Dick Rock* at the east edges of the province. Another notorious rock is *Drunken Dick,* where the traveler will learn, firsthand, the horrors of alcoholism. For the modest traveler, there is plain *Mad Rock* near Halifax. Nearby *Croak Rock* provides background sound effects for *Mad Rock* gazers. An unusually desirable rock is *Wippy Rock,* conveniently located near Halifax. Nova Scotia has a *Blond Rock,* perhaps because gentlemen prefer them, but the province also has a *Cuckold Rock* even though such rocks are not preferred by gentlemen. Nova Scotia has dirty rocks, like *Grime Rock,* and rocks that just lie there and don't do anything, like *Lump Rock.* Visitors can have an illigitimate Nova Soctia vacation at *Bastard Rock.*

Visitors taking a passion path tour of Nova Scotia will want to reach *Pretty Mary Lake* and *Spawn Hole.* Members of the optional *John Island* excursion will want to also take in *Isle Madame.* Most tour busses stop to allow photographic opportunities of bathing beauties at *Big Ass Lake.* Modest passion tour members may wish to get off the busses at *Modesty Cove,* because one hardly knows what to say about the goings-on at the last stop, *Rear of Ball Creek,* near Sidney.

Not all parts of Nova Scotia are equally attractive. A tour of Nova Scotia's less attractive destinations begins at *Slob Point.* From there the tour travels to *Half Bald Island,* where visitors can watch rangers comb spruce logs over the island's bare spot to keep up appearances. The "unattractive tour" includes a visit to the trio of *Grimm Lakes* not far from Digby. One would have thought a *First Grimm Lake* would have been sufficient for any province, but no, Nova Scotia has a *Second Grimm Lake* and a *Third Grimm Lake.* This province also has a plain old *Dirty Creek.* Both *Grimm Lake* and *Dirty Creek* excursions are followed by a stop at *Bath Brook.* An extra advantage of the "unattractive tour" of Nova Scotia is that there is no need to pay capital city prices for hotel accommodations. Economical room and board is provided to tour members, at *Shanty Hill* not far from Halifax. Finally, no tour of Nova Scotia's less attractive destinations is complete without a visit to the town of *Low Point.* There, visitors can enjoy a game of golf at the *Low Point* golf course.

Lake Debate is arguably the best outrageous lake in Nova Scotia. Canadian politicians avoid *Frankville* when they visit Nova Scotia. They much prefer to rejuvenate by splashing about in *Hypocrite Brook* and *The Run-around Brook.*

Nova Scotia's mental health facilities are the talk of the continent. Lunatics of Scottish ancestry are confined on *McNutt Island.* Ghosts of the mentally ill frequent *Loonhaunt Lake.* Travelers can visit *Crazy Kate,* near Mushaboom. If Kate is not crazy enough, travelers might enjoy visiting *Mad Moll Rock.* Kate and Moll may have gone mad because of the nearby booms, *Mushaboom* and *Boom Rock.* Visitors who find themselves suffering from mild melancholia will enjoy *Little Moody Lake.*

Other unusual, often overlooked places to see are *Ecum Secum, Foul Ground, Grosse Spit,* and *Bad Neighbor Shoal.*

Ontario

"The Economic Heartland"

True Facts and Silly Stats

Population: 8,625,107
Area: 412,582 sq. mi.
Capital: Toronto
Largest City: Toronto
Province Motto: We Are Not Detroit
Origin of Province Name: Indian word meaning, "Do you think the Whites will stay the weekend?"
Best Athlete: Wayne Gretzky
Best View: CN Tower, Toronto
Best Museum: Royal Ontario Museum, Toronto
Major Tourist Attraction: Niagara Falls

Outrageous Tour Highlights

Ontario is the location of Canada's largest city, Toronto. It also has the capital of Canada, Ottawa. The province has generated a vast amount of wealth from minerals, manufacturing, and the timber industry. Toronto has a number of attractions, including: the CN Tower (the world's tallest free-standing structure), the Gallery of Inuit Art, the Thomson Gallery, The Art Gallery of Ontario, The Royal Ontario Museum, and the Ontario Science Centre. Ottawa's main attractions are the Parliament Buildings, the National Museum of Science and Technology, and the National Gallery. The leading natural wonder of the province is Niagara Falls, on the U.S./Canadian border. The numerous lakes and vast forests to the north offer many possibilities to outdoor sportsmen.

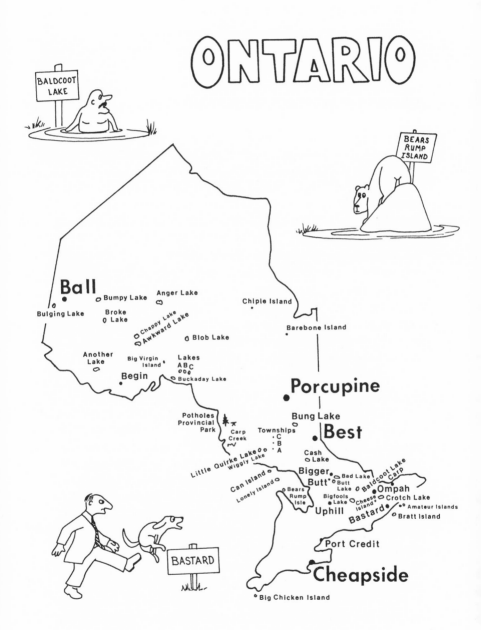

Ontario also has a wealth of outrageous place-names. If you don't know where to begin an outrageous tour of Ontario, a good place to start is *Begin*. You can go on to *Best* for the *Best* vacation.

The yearly freeze and thaw cycle creates remarkable features in Ontario's roads. The most striking examples of these are excavated, preserved, and displayed at *Potholes Provincial Park*.

The remarkable originality of the citizens of this province can be seen in their choice of place-names. Who would have ever thought to name lakes, *Lake A, Lake B, Lake C*, etc. An equal flight of fancy engendered the imaginative names of *Township A, Township B, Township C*, etc. Another burst of creativity resulted in the naming of *Another Lake*.

Known for its great lakes, Ontario has a lake to suit every personality. Try to squeeze into *Bulging Lake* and wiggle into *Wiggly Lake*. On the whole, it is probably best to avoid *Bad Lake*. For those who feel awkward in the water, there is *Awkward Lake*, and for those who are feeling mad, there is *Anger Lake*. The gullible should head for *Bigfools Lake*. Old, hairless men should vacation at *Baldcoot Lake*. Don't count on a smooth boat ride at *Bumpy Lake*.

With so many lakes, the province also has many islands. See landforms that are sloppily made and not professional looking at *Amateur Islands*. For a stripped down place with absolutely no accessories, there is *Barebone Island*. Cowards are confined to *Big Chicken Island*. Those who like gazing at the south end of a northbound bear will enjoy *Bears Rump Island*.

Things are not always easy in this province. For example, the mayor of *Uphill*, has an *Uphill* career. People complain at *Carp Creek*. If you want to see what they complain about, visit *Bastard*. Hear the *Bastard* politicians tell how their administration will make a better *Bastard*. Needless to say, there is no legitimate theater in town.

For those who can afford it, there is *Buckaday Lake*, and for those who can't afford it, there is *Broke Lake*. The economical can stay at *Cheapside*. The best place to dock on an outrageous financial tour is *Port Credit*.

Ontario runs the amours gamut from *Crotch Lake* to *Butt Lake* and *Big Virgin Island* to *Chipie Island*. End your trip at the remarkable town of *Butt*, where the town motto is "Everyone is behind you."

Other unusual places are *Blob Lake, Ompah,* and *Little Quirke Lake.*

Prince Edward Island

"The Smallest Province"

True Facts and Silly Stats

Population: 122,506
Area: 2,184 sq.mi.
Official Capital: Charlottetown
Largest City: Charlottetown
First European Explorer: Jacques Cartier
Province Motto: We Have All the Smelts You Can Eat
Province Industries: Butter, Cheese, Potatoes, and Lobster
Booster Slogan: We Have a Better Climate Than New Brunswick
Provincial Squeeze: Most Densely Populated Canadian Province
Major Tourist Attraction: Prince Edward Island National Park

Outrageous Tour Highlights

Prince Edward Island is the smallest province in Canada. It has a rural and mostly agricultural society. The only town of significant size is Charlottetown, the province capital. The province has become an important destination for vacationers searching out the small picturesque fishing villages, the charming rural areas, and miles of sandy beaches. Prince Edward Island is famous for its lobsters and for the writer Lucy Maud Montgomery, the author of *Anne of Green Gables*.

Prince Edward Island is noted for its straightforward and direct citizenry. For example, it's "wham bam, thank you

PRINCE EDWARD ISLAND

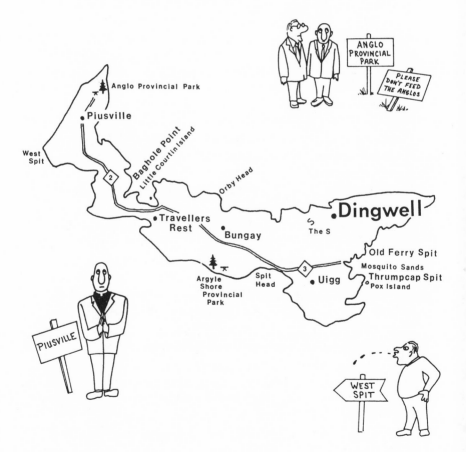

ma'm," at *Little Courtin Island.* Of course, this sort of carrying on doesn't happen at *Piusville. Baghole Point* has its name from the local people's direct but impolite habit of pointing at a bag's hole. One of the few exceptions to their directness is *The S.* We are left to guess what the "S" stands for.

Expectoration is important on Prince Edward Island, as it is in most of Canada. *Spithead,* took its name from the first site among colonial settlements where spitting was permitted. A stay at *West Spit* is usually uneventful, unless of course, there is a strong wind out of the west. At any rate, it is certainly preferable to *Old Ferry Spit.* Even the new stuff is nasty. *Thrumpcap Spit* should also be avoided, whatever a thrumpcap should turn out to be.

The park system of this province is justly famous. The experienced tourist will never miss a chance to visit *Anglo Provincial Park.* At this park you can observe free-ranging provincial Anglo-Saxons interacting in this pristine ecological setting. Hunting by French-speaking Canadians in this preserve is prohibited. You may avail yourself the pleasure of observing the natives washing their Argyle socks in the surf at *Argyle Shore Provincial Park.*

Canada is noted for its important contributions to NATO defenses in the North Atlantic. *Mosquito Sands* is the Canadian equivalent of the U.S. government's proving grounds at White Sands. At *Mosquito Sands,* the Canadian government engages in top secret experiments developing mosquitos for use in the next war. Training of watch mosquitos, guard mosquitos, and attack mosquitos goes on under tight national security. A special detachment of mosquito mounties is stationed on the beaches to guard the facility from curious tourists.

Other unusual localities are *Pox Island* and *Orby Head.*

Quebec

"A North American France"

True Facts and Silly Stats

Population: 6,438,403
Area: 594,860 sq. mi.
Capital: Quebec
Largest City: Montreal
Province Motto: I Bet You Speak English in the Closet
Rank: Canada's Largest Province
Origin of Province Name: Indian word meaning, "You won't believe it, but these people eat snails!"
Most Famous Marriage: Liz Taylor and Richard Burton
Best Art Gallery: Musée des Beaux Arts, Montreal
Most Beautiful City: Quebec City
Most Famous Building: Chateau Frontenac, Quebec City
Major Tourist Attraction: Quebec City

Outrageous Tour Highlights

Quebec is the largest province of Canada. French is the language of 80 percent of the population in this province. The largest city in Quebec is Montreal, and economic center and home of a number of fine galleries and museums. The Laurentian Mountains north of Montreal compose one of the largest ski areas in North America. Quebec City is one of Canada's most beautiful cities and is filled with historic architecture. It includes the only walled city in North America.

Quebec is a bastion of French culture in North America. Enjoy great conversations with people who can talk about any topic off the top of their head, at *Cap Chat*. Or if you just want to

QUEBEC

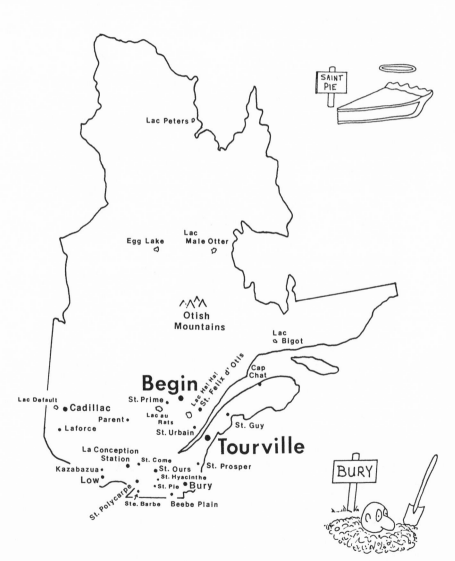

SAINT PIE

Lac Peters

Egg Lake

Lac Male Otter

Otish Mountains

Lac Bigot

Cap Chat

Begin

Lac Hai Hai

St. Felix d'Otis

Lac Default

Cadillac

St. Prime

Lac au Rats

Parent

St. Guy

Laforce

St. Urbain

Tourville

La Conception Station

St. Come

Kazabazua

St. Ours

St. Prosper

BURY

Low

St. Hyacinthe

St. Pie

Bury

St. Polycarpe

Ste. Barbe

Beebe Plain

see the sights, visit *Tourville*, a place made with the tourist in mind.

The saintly nature of the province is legendary. There is *St. Pie* for those who seek the best in religious cooking. *St. Prosper* is for those who do very well in the religious business. *St. Hyacinthe* is named for the only flower child in the 1960s to be canonized. *St. Barbe* must have been named after some other Barb than the one we knew. *St. Guy* is ardently sought out by single women, but we think it is sexist of the province not to have a St. Gal. At *St. Ours*, they have gotten their saint, it's up to you to get your own. They have really fine saints at *St. Prime*. And, *St. Come* is clearly for new arrivals.

Don't mess with the French-speaking police at *Laforce*. At *Low*, you can enjoy the *Low* nightlife during the evening, and the ordinary *Low* life during the day. The town motto is, "If you want to get lower than *Low*, you've got to bring a shovel." Which brings us to *Bury*. Enjoy the local gossips digging up the dirt at *Bury*.

Quebec lacks for nothing. For those who lack faults, there is *Lac Dufault*. For those who lack rats, there is *Lac au Rats*. Those lacking prejudice should stay at *Lac Bigot*. It is bad times for female otters at *Lac Male Otter*, and men are missing something at *Lac Peters*. You don't know the good times you are missing at *Lac Ha! Ha!*.

Many tourists visit *Kazabazua* wondering what kazabazuas are. When you see the kazabazus on the local women, you'll know.

Some other unusual, often overlooked places are *La Conception Station*, *Otish Mountains*, and *Egg Lake*.

Saskatchewan

"The Wheat Province"

True Facts and Silly Stats

Population: 968,313
Area: 251,700 sq. mi.
Capital: Regina
Regina's Original Name: Pile O'Bones
Largest City: Saskatoon
Province Motto: Can You Lend Me Money for a Train Ticket Out of Here
Largest Crop: Wheat
Economic Base: Wheat
Province Renaissance Man: Grows barley and rye, as well as wheat
Most Famous Tourist: Sitting Bull
Those in the Province Who Believe They Have Found Utopia: Hutterites
Major Tourist Attractions: Prince Albert National Park

Outrageous Tour Highlights

Saskatchewan is covered by vast areas of farm fields in the south and sparsely populated forest wilderness in the north. Southern Saskatchewan has spectacular vistas of grasslands and badlands. Northern Saskatchewan has seemingly unending coniferous forests sprinkled with sparkling lakes. There are few roads in the north, and the area primarily attracts visitors interested in hunting, fishing, and canoeing.

While Saskatchewan is known for its remarkable lakes, its outrageous lakes are certainly more colorful. Yacht with the

SASKATCHEWAN

Wandering Lakes
Hicks Lake
Singed Dog Island
STINK LAKE
Unknown Lake
Crimes Lake
Waitville
TINY
Flin Flon Lake
Slime Lake
Bar Lake
Belcher Lake
Inch Lake
Wormworth Lake
Pimple Lake
Funk Lake
Bootleg Lake
Meaney Lake
Bug Lake
Keg Lake
Bland Lake
Big Sucker Lake
Fartown
16
Hoodoo
Gyp Lake
Reserve
Reward
Primate
Smuts
Tiny
Superb
Romance
OGLE
Renown
The Bad Hills
Bad Lake
Stink Lake
Wee-Two Beach
Freefight Lake
High Point
Snakehole Lake
Parkbeg
Surprise
1
Pinkie
Leakville
Chick Lake
The Dirt Hills
Forget
Ogle
Fertile
Climax

sophisticated set at wondrous *Stink Lake.* Have a slick time at spectacular *Slime Lake.* Fishermen love *Bug Lake,* where they can catch their limit of bugs every time. *Snakehole Lake* is a wonderful place for those anglers dropping a line into a snakehole. Then there is *Wormworth Lake,* just to see what a lake worth a worm is like. Even bad swimmers can make it from one end of *Inch Lake* to the other.

For drinkers there are a number of key lakes to visit. There is *Bar Lake,* Bootleg Lake, Keg Lake, and *Belcher Lake.* The final destination on this intoxicating lake tour of Saskatchewan is *Wee-Too Beach.* Ultimately, if you plan to spend time in this fine province you can travel to *Wandering Lakes.* Hopefully, you will find one before they wander away.

No trip to Saskatchewan is complete without arriving at *Renown.* Anyone who lives in the place is a *Renown* citizen, and any person who gets elected is a *Renown* government official. They have *Renown* juvenile delinquents in their *Renown* jail. If *Renown* people are not enough for you, there is *Superb,* which is full of *Superb* citizens. Those in *Superb* who can't do anything right are known as *Superb* incompetents. *High Point* will be the high point of your vacation dreams. It will certainly beat *Bad Lake* and *The Bad Hills.* For a short vacation, *Tiny* has its attraction. It's easy to be a big shot in *Tiny,* and anyone with any brains at all can be a *Tiny* intellect. The *Tiny* children go to a *Tiny* school, where the *Tiny* class size is considered exemplary.

Those wanting a *Surprise* vacation can find it north of Highway 1, in southwestern Saskatchewan. The visitor can be taken by *Surprise* to see the neighboring sights. If the town annexes land, it could become a big *Surprise.*

For those seeking a quiet stay, there is *Reserve.* There you can see *Reserve* punk rockers attend *Reserve* punk rock festivals.

Those searching for *Romance* in Saskatchewan will find it. Dirty old men, not satisfied by singular smut, can find the plural at *Smuts.* Visitors who like to watch *Fertile* women can go on to *Ogle.* Those wanting to monkey around can head for *Primate.*

Other unusual, often overlooked places to see are *The Dirt Hills, Singed Dog Island,* and *Flin Flon Lake.*

Yukon

"Gold Rush Territory"

True Facts and Silly Stats

Population: 10 Eskimos, 20 Indians, 400 bears, Sergeant Preston and his dog Yukon King

Area: 184,931 sq. mi.

Capital: Whitehorse

Largest City: none

Climate: nine months of winter and three months of bad ice skating

Territorial Motto: When You Consider Marrying a Bear, You've Been Here Too Long

Industry: Gold Mining

Origin of Territorial Name: Indian word meaning, "It has gotten so cold, I will never be able to reproduce."

Territorial Formal Wear: Plaid Shirt and Black Tie

Last Good Business Season: 1898 Gold Rush

Major Tourist Attraction: The Chilkoot Trail

Outrageous Tour Highlights

The Yukon is graced with some of the most spectacular scenery in North America. There are several highways into the area, and it is far more accessible than the neighboring Northwest Territories. The Yukon has magnificent mountain vistas including several of the highest mountain peaks in Canada. The history of the territory is as colorful as its scenery. This was the location of the famous Klondike gold rush. Dawson City retains the nineteenth-century architecture of the gold rush days.

The Yukon has something for everyone. Depending on

your political taste, you can travel down *Conservative Trail* or tour *Liberal Ridge.* You can run naked up *Streak Mountain.* Swim in your underwear at *Undie Creek.* Visit *Finger Mountain,* where the gesture is everything. Those needing further insults can go to *Rude Creek.*

There are things to avoid on any trip. Save yourself some disappointment and skip *Disappointment Glacier.* Frankly, it would be a mistake to visit *Mistake Mountain.* However, *T-Bone Glacier* is a tasty alternative. We also recommend avoiding *Almost Lake* in favor of visiting a real lake. And, *Runt Creek* should be skipped in favor of nearby full-size streams.

For those who want to sit down on a mountain there is *Chair Mountain,* and for those who wish to do the same in a stream there is *Big Sitdown Creek.* Have you ever wanted a rental swamp? If so, check out the rates of the rental company at *U Slough. Walking River* is for people who have never seen a waterway stroll by. *Beloud Post* and *Noisy Creek* are not for those seeking a quiet getaway.

Marvel at the Yukon's only zoning law, at *No Sheep Creek.* Put a fish on your hook and catch bait at *Worm Lake.* Women should be sure to visit a *Moosehide* beauty parlor and receive a famous *Moosehide* facial.

Place-names relating to food and drink are dear to the hearts of the province citizens. *False Teeth Creek* can easily be reached after visiting *Rockcandy Mountain.* Those from *False Teeth Creek* have a strong attraction toward *Mush Lake.* For people on the go, there is *Prune Mountain.* Drinkers who visit *Champagne* bars, will get beer at *Champagne* prices. Non-drinkers will want to join the *Champagne* temperance league.

Visit *Mount Queen Mary.* This locality was named for a scandalous historical event involving the Royal Family and a cabin full of lonely prospectors. It is the authors' speculation that the phrase "climb every mountain" came from prospectors at *Nipple Mountain.* And finally, do not omit the ever popular *Sayyea Creek, Screw Creek* and *Hump Mountain.*

Other unusual, often overlooked places you should see are *Ping Pong Creek, OK Creek, Too Much Gold Creek, Tootsee River,* and *Big Thing Creek.*

References

If you are interested in the exact location of a place listed in this atlas, we suggest you consult one of the major road atlases of North America or a local road map.

Because some places are too small or too remote to be included on common road maps, visit a map library and ask for U.S. or Canadian Geological Survey gazetteers of the state or province in which you are interested. These gazetteers are usually catalogued by state or province name. The gazetteers identify maps, such as U.S.G.S. 7.5 minute topographic maps, that provide the locations of the places.

Encyclopedia Britannica World Atlas. Chicago: Encyclopedia Britannica, Inc.

Gazetteer of Canada (Series). Canadian Permanent Committee on Geographical Names. Ottawa, Canada: Surveys and Mapping Branch, Department of Energy, Mines, and Resources.

Geographic Names. Topographic Division. Reston, Virginia: U.S. Geological Survey, National Center.

Rand McNally Road Atlas, United States, Canada, Mexico. Chicago: Rand McNally and Company.

Rand McNally World Atlas. Chicago: Rand McNally and Company.

The World Almanac 1993. Pharos Books. New York: Scripps Howard.

About the Authors

Richard A. Rogers is an archaeologist whose interest in place-names began while doing archaeological research at a Wyoming mining camp named *Armpit.* His wife and coauthor, *Laurine Rogers,* is a biological anthropologist. They live in Des Moines, Iowa, with their baby daughter.